RANGERS GREATS

RANGERS GREATS

DIXON BLACKSTOCK

Foreword by
ANDY CAMERON

JOHN DONALD PUBLISHERS LTD
EDINBURGH

ISBN 0 85976 239 4

The author is grateful to the *The Daily Record* and
Sunday Mail, George Outram and Co., and *Rangers
News* for providing illustrations.

Phototypeset by Swains (Edinburgh) Limited
Printed in Great Britain by Bell & Bain Ltd., Glasgow

Foreword

So, Mr Dixon Blackstock, you have chosen your Nine Favourite
Rangers players who have worn the old Light Blue since the
end of the hostilities with the 'square heads'.

Well, I'm not about to disagree with your choice, for after all
the men you have picked have all done their bit for the Teddy
Bears.

Naw, where we differ, Dixon, is at the point where you
choose to leave out the number one Ranger ever — the Old
Warhorse Jimmy Millar!

Jimmy epitomised everything that a Ranger should be. He
had the spirit that ensured that we would fight till the day is
done.

He was brave where it mattered and he had a bit of cheek
which meant he would try things that ordinary humans could
only imagine or see in a Roy of the Rovers story!

To all of these attributes you can add not a little skill.
Anybody who can trap the ball with his bum in a cup final will
do for me. Wee Ralphie was a rerr player too and I don't argue
with his inclusion in your lot.

However, Brand without Millar is something like a
Woodbine smoker without a cough. You just don't have one
without the other.

While we're at it I'd like to make a case for two or six others
who might have made it on to your subs bench at least. Sammy
Cox for instance was the best tackler I've ever seen. When
Sammy tackled you, you stayed tackled.

Then there was Big Ben — Willie Woodburn. When you see
what's going on in the game today and then think back to Willie
being banned for life . . . well let's just say that Willie, compared
to some of today's thugs, looks like the tooth fairy!

Rangers have always had players who had personality, like
wee David Wilson. The blond hair flowing in the wind as he

headed for goal and if he was tackled in the centre circle remember how he always ended up in the box and was shouting 'Penalty' as he fell?

And what about Super Cooper? Oh, ah know that Davie blows hot and cold, but when he starts one of those runs of his the whole stadium buzzes and it just explodes if Davie plants one of his specials in the pokie à la Skol Cup Final in October 1987.

If there had been no net that day the ball would have landed in Ru'glen.

Davie isn't the only one of today's team who could be in my squad. Ian Durrant is one of the best young players in Europe and when he matures off the park as well as on, he'll be World Class.

Big Terry Butcher must get a mention, for let's face it the Teddys have just gone a half season without his presence in the team and we've performed more like the Rangers from Cambuslang than Ibrox.

Well, Dixon, you paid your money and you made your choice, and as I stated earlier anybody who pulls on that jersey is great to me, and between us we haven't even scratched the surface.

When you look at our lists and see the names that are missing such as Tam Forsyth, Sandy Jardine, Alex MacDonald, Willie Thornton and Tiger Shaw . . . Here, maybe you should have made it your NINETY Great Rangers.

Andy Cameron

Contents

Greats from the past: Scottish Cup winning pool of season 1929-30. They also won the Glasgow Cup, the Charity Cup and the Scottish League Championship. Back row: D. Meiklejohn, T. Marshall, A. Archibald, J. Fleming, T. Hamilton, J. Buchanan, T. Craig. Front row: J. Kerr (trainer), G. Brown, D. Gray, R. Mcdonald, T. Muirhead (capt.), R. McPhail, R. Hamilton, W. G. Nicholson, A. Morton, and W. Struth (manager).

Introduction

Even before this book ever reached the stage of publication, I had a fair sample of the reaction anyone can expect if they are brave enough to select just nine Rangers Greats.

When friends heard my list of names, I was invariably greeted with 'but how could you miss out so and so?'

The alternative names supplied would fill another three books. Sammy Cox, Willie Waddell, Willie Thornton, Jock Shaw, Willie Woodburn, Ian McColl, Billy Simpson, Jimmy Millar, Willie Henderson, Colin Stein, Ron McKinnon, Davie Cooper . . . right on up to the present crop of English stars like Terry Butcher and Chris Woods.

I've no doubt, the readers will add a few more.

But it all comes down to choice. The players I saw, admired, met and liked over the years as first of all a young football enthusiast, then a young sports reporter and now a definitely not-so-young writer for the *Sunday Mail.*

The story, and the glory of Rangers, is jam-packed with legendary names. Going back for more than a century now.

To go with the glittering names came the glittering prizes.

League champions 38 times. Scottish Cup Winners 24 times. Holders of the League Cup 15 times. Plus of course winners of the European Cup Winners' Cup in 1971-72.

These trophies were won by great players on the pitch; astute management off it; and the support of the most fanatical fans in the world.

Naturally there has been argument, controversy, sometimes bitterness and on a couple of occasions tragedy. Twice Ibrox has been the scene of horrible accidents that have resulted in numbing death tolls — 25 people died when part of the wooden terracings collapsed in April, 1902.

And even more tragically 66 lives were lost in the disaster on the exit steps after the New Year game against Celtic on January 2, 1971.

There is little chance of a repeat of that nowadays in the safety-conscious Ibrox, where the 45,000 capacity crowd enjoy the best, most modern stadium in the country.

The building of the new £12 million stadium was the dream of former club winger, manager and director Willie Waddell, who arrived at Ibrox as boss in December 1969 and proceeded to drag the club out of the past and into the future inside the space of a few dramatic years.

Willie Waddell was only the fifth manager in the history of the club at that point, replacing Davie White who had in turn succeeded Scot Symon.

Symon, like Waddell a former Rangers player, was thirteen years in what must be one of the toughest jobs in football anywhere in the world. Rangers fans are not noted for their patience when success is slow in coming.

But even Symon's lengthy spell seems insignificant when compared with the fact that HIS predecessor, the famous Bill Struth, held the post for thirty-four years . . . and before that the club's first manager-secretary William Wilton was in power from 1899 till he died in a drowning accident in May 1920.

Under Wilton Rangers won ten league championships and four Scottish Cups.

In thirty-four years in Struth's control the club won eighteen League flags, and ten Scottish Cups, including twice having a hat-trick of success. Plus eighteen Glasgow Cups and twenty Charity Cups when those trophies meant something.

There are times when it's hard to separate the myth from the man with regards to Struth. He was never a footballer, coming to Ibrox initially as trainer from Clyde following a career as a professional runner.

But he certainly created an aura of power, and was clearly a shrewd psychologist. Tales of how he kept tight control on events at Ibrox are boundless.

Yet it would appear that he never tried to burden his teams with too much in the way of tactics.

'He would never tell you what to do — but he could tell you what NOT to do', recalls Bob McPhail, a great inside forward in the '20s and '30s at Ibrox.

The dapper Struth kept a wardrobe full of suits in a separate dressing room at Ibrox. And kept a tight grip on his players by virtue of what must have been a wide-ranging 'spy' system which could tell him who was up to what.

He insisted on a high standard of dress. In fact, it's told that he even made the rebellious Torry Gillick, a fine player but also a character with a mind of his own, turn up at Ibrox in the then obligatory bowler hat.

However, it's also said that Gillick would travel to Ibrox by bus wearing his favourite bunnet, carrying the bowler in a bag to be donned for the last few hundred yards of the journey to the ground.

Right from their beginnings last century, Rangers have managed to produce a succession of top international players.

As far back as 1888 Donald Gow was captaining Scotland against England . . . and was followed in that position by Jock Drummond, Nick Smith and Jacky Robertson by the turn of the century.

That tradition has been maintained for decade after decade, and even at this moment there are youngsters like Ian Durrant and Derek Ferguson who look set to be important players for Scotland in the coming years.

Along with the likeable Ally McCoist, who has survived some early doubts about his determination to make it really big at the top level. I was among the doubters by the way, but Ally made me admit I was wrong — so much that I have no hesitation in including him in my list of Rangers Greats.

Ally is the latest in a long line of goal-scorers with Rangers to discover that it is the hardest job in football. There is no pleasing the public at times. Last week's hat-trick is forgotten if you miss a couple of sitters this week.

Ralph Brand, Max Murray, George McLean, Jim Forrest, Derek Grierson . . . all know what like it is to be at the sharp end. Both in a playing sense, and also with regard to criticism from press and public.

My choice of nine players was made from the years that began when football resumed after the Second World War.

So that ruled out the pre-war legends like Alan Morton, who

played eleven times against England between 1921 and 1932. Also men like Sandy Archibald, Bob McPhail and Davie Meiklejohn, rated by the late Celtic chairman Sir Robert Kelly as the 'greatest Ranger of all, and a most inspiring captain.'

These were the stars who helped Rangers and Bill Struth dominate Scottish football in the years between the wars, with generally only Celtic able to break the Ibrox grip.

Between 1918 and 1939, a total of twenty-one years, Rangers won the championship sixteen times; Celtic took the flag four times and Motherwell were the only outside team to stop the monopoly of the Old Firm when they wrested the honour in 1932.

The very beginnings of Rangers are shrouded in a bit of doubt. The romantic official version gives the tale of a group of fit young men from Gareloch, rowing for pleasure on the Clyde, stopping to watch a game on Glasgow Green in July 1873.

And deciding to form their own team called Rangers, a name chosen from an English RUGBY side.

Some of that contains truth; some of it is fiction. More zealous researchers like Robert McElroy, founder in recent times of a monthly booklet called 'The Rangers Historian', now point to evidence which shows that the club was actually formed a year before the official date of 15 July, 1873.

And it was a walk in a park in the West End of the city which sparked off the idea as four youngsters talked about the way football was becoming the most popular sport in the country.

Their names were Willie McBeath, Peter Campbell and the brothers Peter and Moses McNeill. It was Moses, then only 16, who came up with the name Rangers.

Rangers were launched, and survived some early financial troubles in the first few years of the club to become the wealthiest, best-supported team in the country.

They were among the original founders of the Scottish League along with Celtic, Third Lanark, Hearts, St Mirren, Dumbarton, Renton, Cowlairs, Cambuslang, Vale of Leven and Abercorn.

And that first League Championship in 1890-91 was to finish with joint champions — Rangers and Dumbarton. This was decided after the pair had finished level on points, and ended up drawing 2-2 in a play-off game at Cathkin on May 21, 1891.

It was to be eight years before the title was claimed again. And this time there could be no question of sharing.

The Rangers team of 1898-99 went through the entire 18-match League programme by winning EVERY GAME.

They scored 79 goals and conceded only 18 and won the flag by 10 points from Hearts.

Rangers were off and running, and took the title for the next three years as well.

The Scottish Cup was more of a problem. As early as 1877 they reached the Final, and lost in the second replay against the then mighty Vale of Leven. Two years later the same teams met again and drew 1-1.

But angered by an offside decision which they felt deprived them of their rightful victory, the Rangers team refused to turn up for the replay.

And while Vale were claiming the Cup, Rangers were having a day out at Ayr races!

It was to be another fifteen years before Rangers made another Final — beating Celtic 3-1.

The names of those early heroes may have faded now, but they were legends in their time. R.C. Hamilton, Neilly Gibson, Tom Hyslop, Alec Smith and Nick Smith were all international players.

Nick Smith, a powerful full back from Darvel in Ayrshire, was a favourite of the fans, and they were shocked when at the age of 31 he died in hospital in Kilmarnock from enteric fever . . . just a few days after his wife, who had nursed him for weeks earlier, had also died.

Incidentally, for winning that first Scottish Cup the players were awarded a bonus of three guineas.

The club went into the twentieth century as Rangers Football Club Limited, a decision reached on March 27, 1899.

Rangers ushered in the new era, and the new century, as Scottish champions. They were poised to become one of the great names in football . . . as were rivals Celtic, who beat Rangers 2-1 in a decider for the championship in 1905 and proceeded to win the title for the next five years.

It was early into the twentieth century that Rangers ran into the 'hoodoo' years in the Scottish Cup. After the 1903 victory over Hearts — 2-0 after two earlier draws — the trophy was to elude Rangers for the next twenty-five years.

League championships galore; the same with Glasgow and Charity Cups. But the Scottish became elusive. Rangers lost out in finals to Celtic, Third Lanark, Partick Thistle and Morton over the years before the jinx which had lasted quarter of a century was banished with the historic 4-0 win over Celtic.

A crowd of 118,115 watched the teams go in level at half-time. Then 11 minutes after the break, Celtic's Willie McStay desperately punched clear a scoring shot from Jimmy Fleming who had met an Alan Morton cross well.

It was a penalty, and one of the truly great Rangers, Davie Meiklejohn, at centre-half that day, accepted the captain's responsibility. He stepped forward and smacked the ball past Celtic's keeper John Thomson.

The doors were open — and Rangers poured through, with Bob McPhail and Sandy Archibald (2) completing a great day.

The Rangers team of that time contained household names: Alan Morton, Davie Meiklejohn, Tully Craig, Sandy Archibald, Andy Cunningham, Bob McPhail and Dougie Gray.

As they faded, they were replaced by a new generation which carried Rangers through the 1930s.

Archie Macaulay, George Brown, Jimmy Smith . . . and the man they called the Prince of Goalkeepers, Jerry Dawson.

Dawson went on to play 545 games for Rangers before his career ended just after the war. He was capped 23 times and won five League medals and two Scottish Cup badges.

He was also one of the game's great characters, endowed with a marvellous sense of humour which I was able to share in many a Press Box when he turned to reporting in his later years.

One of the great stories about him and his humour comes from a wartime game against Hibs at Easter Road when Rangers, down to ten men after Alex Venters had been ordered off, were taking an 8-1 hammering.

At this point the Hibs centre forward Arthur Milne broke through again, rounded Dawson . . . then miskicked in front of the empty goal.

'Have ye stopped trying?' asked Dawson.

After World War Two, Scottish football went through a boom time in crowds as the nation, starved of any real competitive soccer for six years, flocked to see the new generation of stars with Rangers, Hibs, Celtic, Hearts and Aberdeen.

By now, Rangers had entered the Iron Curtain era with a team based on a near-impenetrable defence and fast-raiding forwards.

Before the 1950s were reached, Rangers had won two more of everything — League titles, Scottish and League Cups.

While the defence of Brown; Young, Shaw, McColl, Woodburn and Cox were stopping them . . . Waddell, Thornton and Co. were popping in the winners.

In the 1948 Scottish Cup Final against Morton, a crowd of 129,176 saw the teams draw 1-1 at Hampden. Incredibly, even more turned up for the replay . . . 131,975 watching as Billy Williamson scored the only goal of the game in extra time.

The 1950s brought changes and triumphs in equal share. Five more League titles and two Scottish Cups.

But Bill Struth's 'family' reign was over, and with the return of Scot Symon to Ibrox after successful spells as manager of, first, East Fife and then Preston North End, the old brigade were marching out.

Scot Symon is described elsewhere in the book as 'aloof' and 'not tactically-minded.' Yet people who knew him as a player were impressed by his deep knowledge of the game.

And as manager of Rangers he worked on the principle that THEY were the best team in the country. Therefore his players were the best and didn't have to be told how to play. They wouldn't be in the team if they were not good enough.

Symon set about building his own team, and was also faced with a new challenge . . . Europe. The days of friendly jaunts round the Continent were over, replaced by competitions that were to provide often acrimonious encounters because of contrasting styles and interpretation. And also brought in a tremendous amount of revenue.

Hibs were first into Europe, accepting an invitation to play in 1955-56, despite the fact that Aberdeen were the reigning Scottish champions.

Rangers made their entrance in 1956-57, and found out the hard way from the start that European games were different. They had three tough games against French champions Nice, including a play-off in Paris. In the second leg Rangers had wing half Willie Logie ordered off, apparently for throwing his chin at Nice striker Bravo's fist!

But rough and different though it was — European soccer had arrived. And Rangers' quest for success brought them some great games, and some bitter lessons, along the way.

They lost to Fiorentina over the two legs in the 1960-61 Cup Winners Cup Final; went down 1-0 to Bayern Munich in 1966-67 in the Final of the same tournament and it wasn't until 1971-72 that they finally cracked the European puzzle.

Unfortunately, at their moment of success their fans failed them . . . becoming involved in a pitched battle with the Spanish police after Rangers had beaten Moscow Dynamo 3-2 in a great match in Barcelona.

Long before this, of course, Scot Symon had gone — sacked while his team was leading the table.

But it wasn't insignificant that on the day he left — angered by an approach to him to move out of the manager's seat which was made by a city accountant — Celtic were playing for the World Club championship in South America.

Symon was a victim of Jock Stein's success as much as anything.

He had been manager thirteen years, won six League championships, five Scottish Cups, four League Cups and reached two European finals.

And he had also welded together in the 1960s a team built round the craft and skill of Jim Baxter and Ian McMillan at inside forward; a solid defence and a tremendous striking partnership in Jimmy Millar and Ralph Brand.

There are people who will tell you that side was as good as anything which had worn the Ibrox colours at any time in the past.

His assistant Davie White was moved up; but it was not a move that succeeded and the former Clyde boss lasted just two years before Rangers sacked him and brought in Willie Waddell.

It was a popular move. Waddell, working by then as a sports journalist, had been an Ibrox hero as a player. He had then led Kilmarnock to a remarkable League championship in '64-65, taking the flag by winning 2-0 against all odds at Tynecastle in the last game of the season with Hearts confident of success . . . and the title for themselves.

Then Waddell, noted for his direct style as a player and later commentator, introduced a new aspect to his personality . . . a startling change of direction when least expected. He quit Kilmarnock and went back to the typewriter.

That swift ability to catch people by surprise was to be shown again when after the 1972 European success, he suddenly stepped up to be general manager at Ibrox and left the team work to Jock Wallace.

The Waddell-Wallace partnership was to be highly successful; two physically powerful men with one objective — put Rangers right back to the top.

They got an instant pay-off, winning the League Cup against Celtic by gambling that 16-year-old-Derek Johnstone could be a match-winner. Which he was.

And after that came the first League championship for eleven years, the win in 1975 being the last before the introduction of the Premier League. Better was to follow, with the years of 1976 and 1978 bringing all three major Scottish honours to Ibrox.

The style was based on fitness, aggression and tremendous team spirit. Wallace led the way off the field; John Greig was the driving force on the pitch.

So it was considered only natural that he should be heir-apparent to the managerial seat at Ibrox. However, it became vacant before he was ready for the challenge, and the step from the dressing room to the manager's room was too wide for him.

Why this should be remains a mystery. He had a wealth of experience, was sound tactically, particularly for European tics, was steeped in the club and had the admiration of the support who recognised the devotion he had given to Rangers in good and bad times.

It all looked so good in his first season, 1978-79. The League Cup was won by beating Aberdeen 2 - 1 in the Final; the Scottish Cup was eventually won after a tediously drawn-out series of games against Hibs in the Final which only ended after 330 minutes (three games, two sets of extra time) when the unfortunate Arthur Duncan put through his own net.

Rangers also reached the quarter-finals of the European Cup, beating Juventus of Italy and PSV Eindhoven of Holland before going out 2 - 1 on aggregate against Cologne.

But the League was lost to Celtic, with the crunch coming in a game at Parkhead on May 21st which saw the home side come back from a goal down, and with only ten men after the ordering off for Johnny Doyle, to win 4 - 2 with two goals scored in the last five minutes.

There was perhaps a clue in that performance to the reasons for Greig's lack of success: if he had been on the pitch, that might not have happened. But he couldn't find another John Greig.

He tried to shake up the team — buying in players like Ian Redford, Gregor Stevens, Colin McAdam and Jim Bett.

He also sold shrewdly. Never better than the £400,000 Rangers got for Gordon Smith from Brighton.

Ex-Kilmarnock man Smith was a talented but unpredictable player and £400,000 was a great deal for Rangers. Particularly since Brighton boss Alan Mullery had originally come on with an offer of around half that figure, and was eventually talked into doubling his money by Greig.

But he was not so successful when it came to talking his team towards the top prizes. The Scottish Cup was taken again in 1981, thanks to a brilliant performance against Dundee United by David Cooper who was recalled for the replay after a goalless first game.

Ian Redford, who missed a late penalty in that first match at Hampden, was to be more successful in the '81-82 League Cup against Dundee United, lobbing in a late second goal to give Rangers a 2-0 Final victory.

But the team could not find any consistent form in the League.

After getting second place in his first season, Greig could only cajole his team into 5th, 3rd, 3rd and 4th placings in the next four years and eventually he resigned in October 1983, convinced that it was the best move for the club as well as himself.

Rangers were in disarray, so much so that two of Scotland's other top managers, Alex Ferguson of Aberdeen and Jim McLean of Dundee United, declined the manager's post . . . which led to a return to Ibrox for Jock Wallace, who was back in Scottish football with Motherwell.

Jock won the League Cup for Rangers in his two seasons, with Ally McCoist getting a hat-trick against Celtic in the 1983-84 Final.

But a lot of the drive had gone from the big man. And some of his iron discipline, too, according to the likes of Derek Johnstone.

But when he went in April 1986, no-one could have forecast his successor. Rangers had already made sensational changes at boardroom level, the club having been completely taken over by the John Lawrence Group, with the grandson of the former club chairman in total control. However, Lawrence Marlborough has now based his life in the desert heat of Lake Tahoe in America, and the running of the club was handed to David Holmes.

It was Holmes who started a revolution which was to spread beyond Ibrox and involve all of Scottish football.

He boldly went to Italy and recruited Scotland's World Cup midfield man Graeme Souness as player-manager. Which in turn led to even more startling events.

Souness was big-time, and thought big-time. He was also given a fortune to spend and was unhindered or hampered by tradition or lines of demarcation.

If he wanted a top English internationalist, he would get him. So came Terry Butcher from Ipswich; Chris Woods from Norwich; and Graham Roberts from Tottenham.

Others were recruited as well, but without the same success. However, the Souness approach to this is simple: move them on again. A revolving door might come in handy at Ibrox nowadays.

Many traditionalists baulked at the Souness approach. This wasn't GLASGOW Rangers any more — a team instead full of Englishmen and occasional overseas players.

But they are wrong. There are times when Souness and Co. may not get it right, but they are going about it with some style.

Does anyone suppose that the fans of Real Madrid thirty years ago complained about a wee tubby Hungarian called Puskas, South Americans Santamaria and di Stefano and a Frenchman called Kopa?

Rangers are trying to build an 'international' side. And their efforts have not only brought some great players to Scottish football, but have encouraged others to follow smartly.

Maybe it's that above all which has caught out Rangers. Perhaps they didn't think the likes of Celtic and Aberdeen would be prepared to follow them into the market place with such high-spending determination.

CHAPTER ONE

George Young

George Young was the last of the GREAT Rangers captains.

That's not my view — it's expressed by someone with a more detailed knowledge of the contribution that the giant Young made to Rangers . . . Eric Caldow. Says Eric:

'Of course, George was my idol as a boy, and when I broke into the Rangers first team in the early 1950s he was a tremen-

George Young with some of the trophies he collected in a lifetime of success.

dous help. A shrewd observer of everyone's play, concerned about the welfare of younger players and a fierce critic when necessary.'

'He was truly a mgnificent captain. The best there has ever been.'

Considering Caldow succeeded to the prestigious posts of captain in both the Rangers and Scotland international teams . . . just like Young . . . the opinion carries the right credentials.

But is he not doing himself, and the succeeding Rangers capains after Young, a disservice?   'No. I was never a George Young. There will never be another one like him,' declares Eric.

Young was a giant of football in every way.

His 6ft 2in, 15-stone figure bestrode Scottish football at club and national level for more than a decade, from the end of the war until he retired in squalid circumstances in 1957, deprived of the exit he wanted by the petty bickerings of some S.F.A. council members.

Even more than thirty years on, big George recalls the events of May 1957 with a touch of bitterness.

'After our game against Switzerland in Basle on May 19, which we won 2 - 1, I announced that I was quitting football and that my last game would be against Spain in Madrid a week later.'

'That seemed to get right up the noses of some of the then selection committee. Maybe it was just an excuse.'

'A lot of them were gunning for the then S.F.A. secretary George Graham by that time, and I had a very good working relationship with him.'

'In fact, he used to let me get on with running the team — remember we had no manager at that time — and that included not only building up team spirit, but chores like ordering the bus for training etc.'

'Anyway, I had been nursing an injury and after the game against the Swiss we were to meet Germany in Stuttgart and I wanted to give this one a miss to let me fully recover for the game against Spain, which was to be my final appearance.'

'I was out with the boys doing some training before the Germany game, when the chief selector Willie Waters came out and asked me: 'Are you fit to play on Wednesday?'

'The way he asked it really irritated me. I asked him why he was asking this, and if I had ever let Scotland down.'

'All he did was repeat: Will you be fit to play against Germany? I told him no, but I would be ready to face Spain.'

'We beat Germany 3-1, and moved on to Madrid. Then the day before the game, the selectors came into the dining room and announced the team. I wasn't in it.'

'Fit but not selected' was their description of Young's absence.

The decision not only shattered Young, it knocked the spirit clean out of a Scotland side which had won its last three matches in convincing style.

'One player came to me and said he felt like pulling out of the team — but I told him he had to go out there and play his heart out.'

Whether it was the Young incident or not, the fact remains that the winning streak disappeared from the Scotland set-up. They were 3-0 down inside an hour to the Spaniards and finished up losing 4-1, with Young watching in dismay from the sidelines.

'One of the young players was in tears at half-time. I HAD TO SLAP HIM TO BRING HIM TO HIS SENSES TO GO OUT FIGHTING IN THE SECOND HALF.'

A shoddy end to a shining career. His days with Rangers had ended earlier the same month, with a final appearance in the Light Blue jersey in a Charity Cup semi-final against Clyde at Ibrox on May 4, 1957. But at least he went out on a winning note — leading the side to a 2-0 victory.

So that was the end of George Young as Rangers and Scotland captain.

But what triumphs this giant of a man crammed into his football life.

He played 678 games for Rangers between 1941 and 1957.

He won SIX League championships, leading the side to three of those victories.

He played in four Scottish Cup-winning teams, and twice helped win the League Cup.

And for Scotland he won 55 caps, including two wartime honours against England, and captained the Scots 48 times. Plus, of course, 22 League caps as well.

The statistics are impressive enough. The story of George Young is equally compelling.

Born in Grangemouth in 1922 — where he still lives — he was an avid street footballer by the time he was six.

'Often chased, but never caught by the local bobby', says George.

Not surprising, since George was always a big leggy lad whose long stride carried him around faster than expected.

By the time he was 11, he stood 5' 9" tall and was promptly earmarked as a centre half by the schoolteacher at Dundas Public School.

But it was at full back he was picked for the Falkirk District Schools . . . which in turn led to him being capped for the Scottish schools against Wales and England.

There was a wee inside left in the same Scottish schools side who went on to be a companion at the full international level . . . Billy Steel.

'Billy could have been with me at Ibrox as well,' recalls George.

'I was actually taken to Ibrox as a 15-year-old and put on an amateur form. I think they paid my dad, who was a railwayman in Grangemouth, a couple of quid a week.'

'But then the war came, and all the forms were scrapped.'

'When I was eventually signed in 1941, Billy Steel was made a similar offer but turned it down to go south.'

'Do you know that in 1949 after we beat England 3-1 at Wembley, I tried to get Bill Struth to sign Steelie from Derby', says George.

'He had his chance to join Rangers' was the reply. Struth was not a man who would forgive anyone lightly for snubbing Rangers.

Young was a Kirkintilloch Rob Roy player when Rangers moved in for him.

George Young, all-rounder, deputises for George Niven in goal at Hampden.

Even by then Young, an apprentice marine engineer, was showing an independence of spirit and stubborn regard for his own rights. He had been offered a £10 signing-on fee and £2 a week from Partick Thistle — but demanded the maximum £20 signing-on fee, and didn't get it.

But just to prove that he still had a bit to learn, the teenage Young found himself outsmarted by his junior club officials when the message came that Rangers wanted to see him at Ibrox at 7 o'clock on the evening of September 9, 1941.

George still laughs as he recalls: 'I naturally told the Rob Roy club that I was going to Ibrox, and they said they would meet me at Buchanan Street Station and take me over.'

'Sure enough they did. Then before we set out, they advised me I'd better sign form before we went over to Ibrox. So I did — on the tiles of a 'wally' close beside the station.'

'What I didn't know was that I was signing on as a professional — even though I'd been playing as an amateur with Rob Roy and never got a penny.'

The result of this was when George got to Ibrox, he was signed on the maximum professional fee of £20, while Rob Roy collected £75.

'If I'd stayed an amateur, I would have collected the lot,' says George.

It was a lesson he never forgot, and was to make him a hard bargainer in future years.

Young's early memories of Ibrox are of four stitches in an eye wound in his first reserve game; having his money stolen in a dressing-room raid the next week; and breaking his nose in yet another reserve game a week or so later.

Hardly the best of starts, but within a few more weeks all was forgiven and forgotten.

A telegram to his home on a Friday night told him to report to Ibrox the next day to 'accompany the team' to Hamilton.

'I thought I was along for the experience — but just as we got into Hamilton, the boss told me to get ready to strip. I didn't even have time to get nervous, which was clearly the way Bill Struth planned it all.'

Rangers won 4-1, with the gangling teenager guided through his debut by two astute wing halves in Adam Little and Scot Symon, who simply told him to 'play safe and command the centre of the field.'

He did what he was told, and was launched on the way to a remarkable career.

Wartime football was clearly a strange mixture — Leagues were run in different parts of the country and guest players were forever turning up to play for a variety of teams. Games which finished level were sometimes decided on corners.

In the midst of it all, and with very little real experience, George Young of Rangers became a Scotland player.

And suffered badly at the hands of a multi-talented England side. George played two games inside six months . . . and the Scots lost a total of 12 goals and scored one!

'I was only 20 and had never run into opposition quite like it', recalls George.

The first English attack he faced read: Matthews (Stoke) Carter (Sunderland) Westcott (Wolves) Hagen (Sheffield Utd) D. Compton (Arsenal).

That was an attack which on April 17, 1943 took four off Scotland at Hampden.

If George thought that was bad, worse . . . in fact twice as bad . . . was to follow at Maine Road on October 16.

Young was faced for the first time with one of Britain's great centre forwards . . . Tommy Lawton of Everton. It turned out to be a learning experience.

'I thought he'd brought a ladder,' says George. 'There was never anyone of his height before who could climb for crosses in such a way.'

Lawton scored four times as England, with probably one of their greatest-ever teams, swept to an 8-0 win, leading 5-0 by the interval.

The watching Bill Shankly, who had missed the game because of injury, said at the time: 'Scotland had no chance. That is probably the best England team of all time.'

It was a chastening experience, and it was one George never forgot. It was three years before he was back in the Scotland side, and in the intervening years he set about learning his trade while working in the shipyards at the same time.

And by the time he was back in the national squad again in 1946, George had collected the first of his League championship badges, a League Cup medal and was in the Rangers team which had defeated Hibs 3-1 in the Victory Cup Final at Hampden in 1946.

And, of course, Rangers had entered the era of the Iron Curtain.

Skippered by the rugged Jock 'Tiger' Shaw, Rangers put together a defence in season '46-47, losing only 26 goals in 30 games. And in six seasons they played 180 League games and conceded 180 goals.

'We were hard to beat — but we had great forwards as well', says George. 'We could have defended as much as we liked, but we still needed the likes of Willie Waddell and Willie Thornton to get the goals to win games.'

A feature of Rangers' strategy in those days was Young's 'howitzer' clearances sixty yards upfield.

'But they were not aimless bootings as some people would

suggest,' says George. 'I practised for hours on end so that I could drop the ball on to a space just where I wanted. Like the modern golfers who practise the same thing.'

'It was an attacking move. A lot of teams found themselves under pressure in seconds just when they thought they were building up an attack of their own. We caught many a team with too many players stranded upfield.'

Rangers, of course, were controlled in those early days after the war by the legendary Bill Struth.

'He was a remarkable man, and I became quite close to him after I took over as captain,' says George.

'All those stories about him having dozens of suits in wardrobes at Ibrox are true. He was immaculate, at any given moment of the day.

'And he always insisted the players were turned out properly as well.'

'I can recall a day when a wee boy called Tom Robertson, a provisional signing, came in with a velvet jacket and shoes with silver buckles.'

'Struth came into the dressing room, and looked at the jacket on the peg . . . which were so high even I had to stand on a bench to get to them . . . then looked at the shoes. He reached up and took the jacket down with his walking stick, and asked who owned it.'

'After training the buzzer went and wee Tom was summoned upstairs. We never saw that jacket or those shoes again.'

Struth took a great interest in his players, and what they were doing.

'He had an amazing army of informers who could tell him all that was going on,' says George.

'I can remember one Saturday night going skating in Falkirk instead of going to the dancing as normal. By the Monday I was upstairs and told to stay away from skating, which could be dangerous and 'stick to the dancing at Doaks'.'

'Doaks was the local dance hall in Falkirk. How he knew about it I don't know. But he certainly made sure his players stayed on the straight and narrow.'

Wartime football . . . and Bill Shankly introduces Rangers Waddell and Young.

'He had a human side, too. He wouldn't let any of us drive to Ibrox in case of accidents. We had to take the train. Well, quite a few of us from the Falkirk area, including Jerry Dawson, used to take the car into Glasgow, park it round the corner from Copland Road subway and walk to the ground.

'What we didn't know was the yard we were parking in belonged to the Rangers chairman Bailie Wilson and Bill Struth soon found out.'

The Rangers team abounded in talent and was rich in character.

One such was inside forward Torry Gillick, back at Ibrox for his second stint after a spell with Everton.

'They used to say Torry only came back so he could run his greyhounds at the Albion', says George. 'Apparently in the days before the war, Bill Struth insisted that Torry wear a bowler hat like the rest of the players.'

'Torry would travel back and forward on the bus in his bunnet, with the bowler in a bag, then put it on for the last few hundred yards' walk to the stadium.'

'Jerry Dawson was a great character as well as a magnificent goalkeeper. I can recall one wartime game against Hearts when he put up the shutters in the first half, and at the interval Alex Venters turned to him and said: 'Dawson, you've done it for us. Now it's up to us to do it for you.'

'Venters went out and scored twice to win the game for us.'

Training at Ibrox seems to have been a matter of self-discipline and trust in those days after the war. Jimmy Smith, a great character in his own right as a Rangers player in the '30s, was the man in charge.

'Jimmy used to wander around, in his white jacket and puffing his pipe, telling us to get on with it. He always had his dog Sandy with him, and it would join in at times.'

'We used to joke the dog was fitter than us. But basically we all knew what had to be done, what we needed to work on ourselves . . . and we did it.'

Successfully, too, as the records show. Huge crowds followed football, and Rangers, in those years after the war.

'They talk about crowds of a million in one season being something nowadays', says George.

'But I played in four Scottish Cup winning teams at Hampden, and — including two replays — we were watched by 730,836 fans. That was in six games!'

The great rivalry in the late '40s and '50s in the Scottish football was not Rangers and Celtic. It was Rangers and Hibs.

In seven seasons from 1946, Rangers took the title four times . . . and Hibs were runners-up on three occasions. Hibs also won the championship three times, with Rangers in second place every time.

'They used to say that Scotland should pick the Rangers defence and the Hibs attack and take on the world', says George.

'It might not have been a bad idea at that.'

Closest of all the battles between these two clubs was season '52-53.

'We finished all square on 43 points each, but we won on goal average,' recalls George.

Naturally Hibs scored more than Rangers — 93 to 80. Just as naturally, the Ibrox men conceded a lot less than Hibs, losing only 39 goals against Hibs' 51.

'But we only got the title because Willie Waddell scored an equaliser against Queen of South at Palmerston late in the second half,' recalls George.

His international football career picked up again after those two early disasters. He was picked at right back again in Ireland in 1946, which ended 0-0, then came the game that ended 1-1 against England at Wembley on April 12, 1947.

A year, and three more caps later, he was captain of Scotland . . . against England at Hampden. But it wasn't a winning start. Tom Finney and Stan Mortensen scored for England in their 2-0 win and George got a head wound that put him in bed for three days after the match with concussion.

In all, George played nine times against England in his career (after the war games) and found happier results at Wembley than at Hampden.

'We lost against England at Hampden in 1948, '50, '52 and drew in '56', recalls George.

'But we were much more successful when I was captain at Wembley.'

'After the 1-1 draw in 1947, we had 3-1 and 3-2 wins and a 2-2 draw.'

'And we might have got away with a draw in 1957. It was 1-1 with only six minutes to go when Duncan Edwards got England's winner — with a shot diverted off my leg.'

'Even then, he wouldn't have got the chance if Eric Caldow had done what I told him. I wanted him to boot the ball as far into the terracings as he could, but instead he tried to clear upfield and only succeeded in giving the ball to Edwards. And when he hit them from 25 yards they were really travelling. I couldn't get out the way.'

Young was not only captain of Scotland, he acted as manager.

'I built up a very special relationship with the S.F.A. secretary George Graham.'

'He left it up to me to build up the right team spirit, and welcome in new players.'

'I can remember one time he phoned me and told me to go to Central Station and welcome new cap John Hewie of Charlton. I hadn't a clue what he looked like and all I was told was he was a big skinny dark-haired lad.'

'But I did meet him, took him home for a meal with my wife and family, then we went to link up with the rest of the boys.'

Life was clearly more informal in those days, and it was left to Young to take the players out to the Empire Theatre in Glasgow on the eve of the big game to help them relax.

Young's easy relationship with George Graham was in marked contrast to that of his boss Bill Struth.

'They hated each other,' says George. 'Quite often I was caught in the middle. Bill Struth wanted Ibrox to be the No. 1 stadium in the country, used for internationals. George Graham always made sure the games went to Hampden.'

The dislike between two of the leading men in Scottish football was undoubtedly the reason for no Rangers players being present when Scotland went to Switzerland for the 1954 World Cup.

Rangers wanted to tour in Canada and America. The S.F.A. ruled that any Rangers player chosen for the World Cup would have to remain at home and prepare.

The wrangle rumbled for months. Rangers went on tour. No Ibrox men went to Switzerland and Scotland lost both games played, including a 7-0 drubbing by Uruguay.

Young's unique dual role with Rangers and Scotland — he was much more than captain in both camps — didn't stop him having disputes with club and country.

'If I thought something needed to be said, I said it,' says George.

This included his famous 1950 signing revolt when he demanded better terms — and hung out for weeks before finally settling.

'I discovered that Torry Gillick was getting £14 — which was £2 more than the rest of us. I demanded the same.'

'The trouble was that Bill Struth was ill in hospital at the

The long legs of George Young in action against Partick Thistle.

time and I was dealing with the chairman, Bailie John F. Wilson. When I refused terms, he followed me out of the office and said: 'Young, that's the last time you'll walk down these stairs.'

'I was just as shirty back. But in the end, Bill Struth gave me what I wanted and I went to his bedside at hospital on the Saturday morning the season started and signed on.'

'The old devil still had the last word, mind you. Instead of playing that Saturday I signed I was sent to watch a junior player . . . who didn't play in the game I was sent to cover. He might not even have existed. It was just Bill's way of rapping my knuckles.'

Over the years Struth, realising Young's value to the club in the way he presented himself and Rangers, looked after 'Corky' in many ways.

'The expenses were always good,' smiles George.

'Corky', by the way, is the nickname that came George's way after the 1948 Scottish Cup Final in which Rangers beat Morton. At the after-match banquet, a waiter opened a bottle of champagne, then presented George with it as a good luck token — particularly hoping it would help the Scottish international team.

'I decided to carry the cork with me for big games. And it seemed to work for Scotland as well as Rangers,' he says. 'We had won only one full international since the end of the war — 2-0 against Belgium at Hampden.'

'But after I acquired the cork, which was produced pre-match in the dressing room, we beat Wales 3-1 in Cardiff.'

'The rest of the lads began to believe in it. So did I after we beat Northern Ireland, England, France, Nothern Ireland again and then Wales. That cork stayed with me, although we didn't win every game of course.'

One game George remembers was the 8-2 win over Ireland in Belfast.

'Henry Morris of East Fife came into the team, scored a hat-trick and was never capped again', recalls George.

That undoubtedly makes Morris, in percentage terms, the most sccessful Scottish striker of all time!

Just as George Young is Scotland's leading skipper — hav-

Two great captains, Billy Wright of England and George Young of Scotland at Hampden.

ing captained his country 48 times, at one stage playing 34 games in succession.

It was not all brightness and light, of course. Big George remembers well the game that became known as the Battle of Vienna in 1951 when Austria literally kicked their way to a 4-0 victory . . . and the Scots almost had to fight their way off the pitch as the Austrian fans went for them.

'What for, I don't know', says George. 'We had been the victims and we were beaten 4·0 into the bargain, with Billy Steel ordered off for doing absolutely nothing wrong.'

'I was booted on the knee at one point and had to go off for ten minutes. Then at the end of the game Willie Redpath was kicked as well — by a woman spectator.'

Despite his size and physique, Young was never ordered off in his career and in fact was booked only once — by Jack Mowat.

'And that was for remarks I was making toward my own players. How Jack understood me without my teeth and with that Falkirk accent I'll never know.'

George's reputation as a hard but fair player even earned him a place in Sir Robert Kelly's team of all-time Scottish greats (excluding Celtic players) as listed in the Parkhead chairman's book published in the early 1970s.

Young's standing also made him a target for approaches from other clubs.

One came from a prominent English club after Young gave what he himself describes as his 'greatest display' in a 1-1 draw against the English League at Newcastle.

'I equalised with a penalty, stopped everything that came my way, and if I had fallen on my backside I would have trapped the ball under me. It was that kind of night.'

'After it a representative from a big English team offered my £3,000 — a fortune in those days — if I would make a nuisance of myself with Rangers until they agreed to transfer me. I told him he was not on.'

But he was much more interested in the next approach which came, early in the 1950s.

'This is the first time I've told this story', says George.

'We arrived back in Glasgow from a game in Dundee and the Aberdeen manager Davie Halliday was there. He told me Dons were interested in signing me — I was right back at the time — and that several Aberdeen businessmen already had a home picked out and in my name, should the deal be on.'

'My wife and I holidayed a lot up in Aberdeenshire and quite fancied the idea of living there. But Rangers were having none of it. They wouldn't let me go.'

Understandably so, for Young was to fill the captain's gap left when Jock Shaw's career started to wane in season 1950-51.

And more importantly, when Willie Woodburn was suspended in September 1954, Rangers were in the fortunate

George practises his famous howitzer.

position of having a ready-made international centre-half to step in.

To this day, Young believes Woodburn was harshly treated.

'He was sent off five times in his career, and clearly that was punishable. But there are guys getting sent off that number of times inside two seasons nowadays.'

'Willie was an easy target for nigglers — they set out to make him lose the place. Mind you, he did have a fierce temper.'

'I can recall one game in a tour of Denmark where Bobby Brown lost a daft goal, and the spectators were astonished to see this scene of me on the goal line trying to stop our centre half getting at our goalkeeper.'

'Even after the game Woody was fizzing. He aimed a boot at Brown — and unfortunately Bob McPhail, who was acting as tour manager, happened to walk into the way of the missile!'

Young played with, and against, some household names in world football. But the man he rates as the best he ever saw might mean nothing to most people.

'He was a Moroccan called Ben Barek, who played for France against us in Paris in 1948', says George.

'He was as good as Pele. I never saw a better inside forward. I had been warned about him from a former Rangers man John Galloway who saw him in the Middle East. But I never expected anything as good. He was brilliant.'

Before his illustrious career ended, George was to see the start of competitive European football, playing for Rangers in their three European ties against Nice in 1956-57.

'You could tell it was an important development. But I don't think anyone realised just how big European soccer was to become', says George.

'But right from the start there was the problem of different playing styles; different interpretation and temperament and different referees. You had to keep the head in those games abroad, and I can't say I enjoyed them.'

George much preferred the helpings of Cup Finals he received with Rangers in both the Scottish and League Cups.

He remembers the 1949 Scottish Cup Final win over Clyde

Three footballing greats — Young with Don Revie and Bobby Shearer.

with relish — having scored twice from the penalty spot in the 4·1 victory before a crowd of 120,162.

And four years later he found himself starring in an unusual role — goalkeeper.

'It was only for about twenty minutes in the Final against Aberdeen' says George. 'Our keeper George Niven, who had been tremendous, took a bad head knock.'

'We were leading 1·0 at the time, and I managed to keep everything intact until the interval. But I was happy to see a patched-up George Niven come back for the second half.'

Aberdeen did get an equaliser 10 minutes from the end of this game watched by 129,762 fans. And another 113,700 were at Hampden to see Billy Simpson take the Cup with a low shot in the 42nd minute.

'Great games, great days. I enjoyed every minute of it and had no regrets about retiring. Only about the way the end came for me with Scotland,' says George.

After finishing, he concentrated on running his various business interests — the famous Tillietudlum Hotel in Lanark-

shire which he owned for many years; a coffee bar in Glasgow
he shared with George Niven; a plastics business in East Kilbride as well as newspaper and broadcasting work.

He then had a go for three years as manager of Third
Lanark, and succeeded in making Thirds a highly watchable
team with a talented forward line which contained Dave Hilley,
Matt Gray and Alex Harley.

'We were the first of the smaller clubs to score 100 goals in
the First Division,' recalls George.

'To get the 'ton' we needed six goals against Hibs at Easter
Road in the last game of the season. I stayed at Cathkin with
the reserves — and left it to the team to get the goals. And they
did.'

He left Cathkin when a power struggle brought in a new
board of directors, sad to go but unwilling to work with people
he didn't like.

Nowadays George spends his time between his Grangemouth home, a caravan up north and winters for three months
in the south of Spain when he can.

The sunshine is necessary. For the years of bumps,
bruises, kicks and stretches have left him a victim of arthritis.

But he is still instantly recognised and recognisable.

'I'll always be George Young of Rangers', he says proudly.
And even soured relationships with the Ibrox club in recent
times, when two tables booked by them at a Testimonial Dinner run for George lay empty, cannot change that.

He remains a keen supporter of local youth football in his
area and for forty years has been chairman of the Erskine Hospital Paraplegic Coach and Comfort fund.

Salute of the Gladiators: Celtic's footballing brothers John and Billy McPhail with Rangers Woodburn and Young.

INTERNATIONAL RECORD

Wartime Internationals

1943

Apr.	England	(h)	0-4
Oct.	England	(a)	0-8

Full Internationals

1946

Nov.	N. Ireland	(h)	0-0

1947

Apr.	England	(a)	1-1
May	Belgium	(a)	1-2
May	Luxembourg	(a)	6-0
Oct.	N. Ireland	(a)	0-2

1948

Apr.	England	(h)	0-2
Apr.	Belgium	(h)	2-0
May	Switzerland	(a)	1-2
May	France	(a)	0-3
Oct.	Wales	(a)	3-1
Nov.	N. Ireland	(h)	3-2

1949

Apr.	England	(a)	3-1
Apr.	France	(h)	2-0
Oct.	N. Ireland	(a)	8-2
Nov.	Wales	(h)	2-0

1950

Apr.	England	(h)	0-1
Apr.	Switzerland	(h)	3-1
May	Portugal	(a)	2-2
May	France	(a)	1-0
Oct.	Wales	(a)	3-1
Nov.	N. Ireland	(h)	6-1
Dec.	Austria	(h)	0-1

1951

Apr.	England	(a)	3-2
May	Denmark	(h)	3-1
May	France	(h)	1-0
May	Belgium	(a)	5-0
May	Austria	(a)	0-4
Oct.	N. Ireland	(a)	3-0
Nov.	Wales	(h)	0-1

1952

Apr.	England	(h)	1-2
Apr.	U.S.A.	(h)	6-0
May	Denmark	(a)	2-1
May	Sweden	(a)	1-3
Oct.	Wales	(a)	2-1
Nov.	N. Ireland	(h)	1-1

1953

Apr.	England	(a)	2-2
May	Sweden	(h)	1-2
Oct.	N. Ireland	(a)	3-1
Nov.	Wales	(h)	3-3

1954

Oct.	Wales	(a)	1-0
Nov.	N. Ireland	(h)	2-2

1955

May	Portugal	(h)	3-0
May	Yugoslavia	(a)	2-2
Oct.	N. Ireland	(a)	1-2
Nov.	Wales	(h)	2-0

1956

Apr.	England	(h)	1-1
May	Austria	(h)	1-1
Oct.	Wales	(a)	2-2
Nov.	N. Ireland	(h)	1-0
Nov.	Yugoslavia	(h)	2-0

1957

Apr.	England	(a)	1-2
May	Spain	(h)	4-2
May	Switzerland	(a)	2-1

CHAPTER TWO

Bobby Brown

Perhaps Bobby Brown's greatest claim to fame is that he was the man who played behind the Iron Curtain for six years.

Not the mythical divide that separated East from West in

Bobby Brown, watched by Jock Shaw, shows a safe pair of hands.

political terms, but the formidable defence which Rangers erected in the heady days after the Second World War.

Young, Woodburn, Cox and Shaw . . . . that was the barrier which prevented the opposition from getting near the elegant, handsome Bobby Brown for season after season. And should anyone get beyond the curtain, they were confronted by a tall, athletic goalkeeper with considerable style and a lot of confidence.

Bobby, now a fit-looking and active pensioner in the Clyde seaside town of Helensburgh, recalls his colleagues with some affection and still a touch of awe.

George Young, a giant in every way: Willie Woodburn, tall, talented and burdened with a fiery temperament; Sammy Cox, a lean, ruthless tackler; and Jock Shaw, the man they called 'Tiger' for very good reasons.

'They were all tremendous players and powerful characters in their own right,' says Bobby. 'They were fierce competitors and didn't like losing even one goal. And if they happened to think it was my fault — they soon let me know in very colourful language.'

'There were quite a few times when Willie Woodburn threatened to throw me into the bath still with my gear on. And he meant it.'

Bobby is obviously of a forgiving nature. For he rates Woodburn, whose career was cut short by a *sine die* suspension in September 1954, as the greatest centre half he has ever seen.

'And that includes players of the past like England's Neil Franklin and Terry Butcher of today,' says Bobby.

'Big Willie had everything. He was commanding in the air, could use both feet with equal ease and could pass and head the ball with great accuracy'.

He was also the owner of a quick temper that was to have him ordered off five times in his career. The last against Stirling Albion was eventually to lead to his life ban.

'You could always see the danger signs when Big Ben was about to strike,' recalls Bobby. 'Usually he was riled by some action against one of our forwards. If someone put the likes of Torry Gillick up in the air, we would all look quickly at Woodburn.'

'If he started plucking angrily at the front of his jersey, we knew that was the signal for bother unless the likes of George Young could get to him quickly and calm him down'.

Even in the dressing room, Woodburn was still to be feared if things had gone wrong. Bobby recalls the scene at Hampden in the 1954 Scottish Cup when Rangers crashed to a sensation 6-0 defeat against Aberdeen in the semi-final at Hampden.

'You could have heard a pin drop in the dressing room,' says Bobby. 'Then a woman spectator happened to pass the window and try to look in, telling her friends this was the Rangers dressing room. That was too much for Woody and his boot was hurled at the window, cracking the glass.'

The years at Ibrox were laden with success and honour for Bobby Brown. But when he originally came to Glasgow as a schoolboy from his home town of Dunipace, this product of Falkirk High School was bound for Queen's Park and the amateur ranks.

'Queen's had a great team in those days. And crowds of around 20,000 watched them. I certainly didn't expect to be plunged into first team football too quickly'.

But the war changed all that.

Queen's at that time had two senior keepers — Egyptian Mustapha Mansour, who was a student in Glasgow, and Gordon Hamilton. When hostilities began, it was back to Egypt for Mansour and Hamilton was soon in the forces.

Which plunged teenager Brown into first-team action in a Southern League game against Celtic at Parkhead on April 13, 1940.

And it was an unforgettable debut for the tall, curly-haired teenager. He lost four goals, saw his team score four and right at the start of the game was handed a never-to-be-forgotten lesson.

'I went up for a swirling cross inside the first minute — and the next thing I knew I was in the back of the net, followed by the ball. Johnny Divers of Celtic helped me to my feet with these words: 'I know it's your first game, son, and you're only a boy. But you'd better learn right now that you f----- punch those kind, you don't try to catch them.'

Ready for action, Brown covers his near post.

Lesson learned, and the game provided an eight-goal thriller for the 50,000 crowd. The teams that day were:

Celtic: Smith; Hogg, O'Neill; Geatons, Lyon, Paterson; Kelly, Lynch, Crum, Divers, Murphy.

Queen's Park: R. Brown; D. Clyne, H Dickson; A. Cross, R.M. Cross, W. Buchanan; J. Gray, A. Aitken, R. Sleigh, W. Browning, W. Wright.

Like so many players, Bobby's football was affected by war service. But he still managed to play eighty-nine games for Queen's in the period 1940-46.

And it was wartime football which was to launch him on his way to the big time. Called up still as a teenager, he joined the Fleet Air Arm at Dartmouth to be trained as a pilot.

He can still show you his log book today, having soloed in the legendary Tiger Moth.

His football career took off, too, with a series of guest appearances for various English clubs such as Chelsea, Portsmouth and Plymouth.

First Lord of the Admiralty at that time was A.V. Alexander, who also happened to be President of Chelsea, and he had the young Brown transferred to the Navy P.E. squad to allow him to play for the Stamford Bridge club.

By 1945, Bobby found himself an international star. He was pulled into the Scotland team to face England at Villa Park on February 5, 1945 — the first of seven wartime caps. He is the last amateur to have been capped for the full Scotland side.

And right well did Petty Officer Bobby Brown play. He couldn't stop Scotland losing 3-2 before a 66,000 crowd in a bomb-scarred ground where the stand seats, which had been hidden away in shelters for safety, were cleaned up and put back in place.

'Brown had arms like an octopus,' declared one English player. And the correspondent from the prestigious *Times* newspaper commented: 'The superior play of their forwards and wing-halves had much to do with the success of England who would have won by more had it not been for some astonishing saves by Brown'.

Even today, Bobby has no hesitation in naming that as his

The youthful Brown in the 1946-47 Rangers line-up.

greatest performance, which earned him hero status from the fans.

The teams that day are worth noting:

England: Swift (Man City); Scott (Arsenal) Harwick ('Boro); Soo (Stoke) Franklin (Stoke) Mercer (Everton); Matthews (Stoke) Brown (Charlton) Lawton (Everton) Mortensen (Blackpool) Smith (Brentford).

Scotland: Brown (Q.P.); Harley (Liverpool) Stephen (Bradford); Busby (Liverpool) Thyne (Darlington) Macaulay (West Ham); Delaney (Celtic) Fagan (Liverpool) Dodds (Blackpool) Black (Hearts) Liddell (Liverpool).

Six more caps followed, including the forgettable 6-1 defeat by England at Hampden before a 133,000 crowd on April 14, 1945.

Bobby's return to civvy life saw him go to Jordanhill College in Glasgow to train as a P.E. teacher .... and depart the amateur ranks for Rangers.

He joined the Ibrox club the same day as Sammy Cox signed from Dundee, and both made their debut forty-eight hours later in a Victory Cup game against Airdrie at Broomfield on May 3, 1946.

It was also the last game for an Ibrox legend, Jimmy Smith, the big bustling centre forward who scored more than 300 League and Cup goals for Rangers.

'Jimmy was a character as well as a prolific scorer,' says Bobby, who still relishes telling the tale of the unpredictable Smith setting off on a mazy run down the right which took him past man after man.

'Scot Symon, our left half and one of the best football brains I ever knew, was with Jimmy all the way waiting for a pass inside. Jimmy came in along the bye-line and Scot was screaming for the ball out of the corner of his mouth. But Jimmy suddenly tried a shot and hit the side-netting instead of cutting it back. 'Why didn't you do the simple thing?' demanded Symon. 'What could be f----- simpler than that?' said Jimmy.

The teams that debut day were:

Airdrie: Moodie; Peters, Hadden; Brown, Brennan, Clapperton; McCulloch, McLean, Aitken, Flavell, Watson.

Rangers: Brown; Cox, Shaw; Watkins, Young, Symon; Waddell, Thornton, Smith, Williamson, Caskie.

Rangers won 4 - 0, with the help of two Willie Waddell goals, and within a month of leaving Queen's Park Bobby Brown was back at Hampden — collecting his first prize with Rangers who beat Hibs 3 - 1 in the Victory Cup Final before an 88,000 crowd.

That was the start of a tremendously successful career for Bobby, but not before he had to go through some turbulent times.

'As an amateur, I had negotiated my own transfer fee, of course, and there was some resentment about that among the other players. The signing on fee was paid to me over a period of time on my wages, which made me the highest-paid player at the club. And incidentally helped build my first home in Stirling.'

'First team wages in those days were £14, plus £2 for a win. I must have been on about three times that for a while, and it rankled with some of the others.'

Flying high, the agile Brown takes down a cross, watched by George Young.

'Also I found the switch to professional football such a big change from Queen's where I was being paid 2s 6d a week travelling costs. After a game with Queen's it was back to Reid's tea room in Gordon Street, Glasgow for a friendly discussion about the afternoon's match, win lose or draw.

'At Ibrox, there was a post mortem about every goal lost. It took me some time to adjust, and there was a lot of confusion between myself and the defenders about cross balls.'

'I was really quite unhappy until November 4, 1946. That was the day I got a letter from a wellwisher who told me that all around him on the terracings he was hearing nothing but praise for my play. I still have that letter and treasure it. It made me feel I had arrived'.

Amazingly, Bobby was NEVER a full-time player with Rangers — preferring to keep on his post as P.E. teacher at Denny High School where one of his respectful pupils and school team players was a certain young man to make a name for himself with Rangers . . . David Holmes!

Bobby trained three nights a week at Ibrox, and there appeared to be no problem with this arrangement for many years, but eventually it created a situation which was to put him out of the first team and then out of Ibrox.

But that was not before he had helped gather in an impressive collection of silverware. He missed only one League game in his first six seasons, and actually played 179 matches in succession.

By the time he departed Ibrox in 1956 he had played in 296 League and Cup matches, including 109 games where he didn't lose a goal.

He won three League championship medals (1947, '49, '50), played in the side that won the Scottish Cup in three years in succession from 1948 and also picked up two League Cup winners badges.

Plus three more full Scottish caps and eight League honours. There would have been more, but for a certain Jimmy Cowan, the Morton goalkeeper who was an outstanding Scottish international success in the late '40s and '50s.

In the triple-crown season of 1948-49 Bobby never missed a match as Rangers took the flag, the Scottish Cup and the League Cup. He played thirty League games, nine League Cup ties and five Scottish Cup matches.

The League Title was taken in dramatic fashion. Going into the final Saturday, Dundee went to Brockville to face Falkirk and needed a win to take the flag. Unexpectedly, they crashed 4-1, and Rangers meantime were beating Albion Rovers by the same score at Coatbridge with the aid of a Willie Thornton hat-trick.

The Ibrox club took the title by a point: with 46 to Dundee's 45. The other statistics tell what was a familiar story in those days. Rangers lost only 32 goals in 30 games, 14 fewer than any other team. They also scored 63 goals . . . . a total passed by five other sides including the unlucky Dundee.

The edge, as always, lay with the Iron Curtain brigade of Brown and Co.

Ask Bobby about his worst moment in those trophy-rich

Bobby Brown, covered by Jock Shaw and George Young, gets down to work.

days and he still squirms as he recalls the 1948 Scottish Cup Final against Morton.

'There was half a gale blowing, and before we went out the manager Bill Struth stressed time and again to me that if we lost the toss and faced the wind I would have to command the box.'

'You can imagine my horror when after only two minutes I came out too far to meet a 40-yard free kick from Jimmy Whyte and the ball swirled over my head AND BOUNDED THREE TIMES before landing in the net, with me tumbling head over heels after it.'

'Although Torry Gillick got an equaliser for us ten minutes later, not a soul spoke to me in the dressing room at half time or full time.'

There was a crowd of 131,975 at the first game, and a

record 129,176 for the midweek return which Rangers won in extra time with a Billy Williamson goal.

'I always reckoned I should have been offered half of the gate money for that replay since a lot of people clearly felt it was me who brought it about,' jokes Bobby.

Crowds were, of course, huge in the happier days after the war as the public thronged to see the stars after the long dark years of strife.

'Everywhere you went there were big gates. And every team seemed to have a handful of great players,' recalls Bobby. 'You would go up to East Fife and 30,000 fans would be there hoping to see Don Emery take a penalty against us.'

'He had the most ferocious shot you've ever seen. Or sometimes never saw.'

'When the Fifers did get a penalty, someone would place the ball on the spot and Don would start his run from the other end of the pitch. As he ran, the crowd crescendo built up to a roar by the time he actually made contact. Usually it went blistering past you with any keeper in his right mind happy to have stayed out the way of it.'

Brown was a handsome, wavy-haired athletic figure who exasperated his colleagues at times by his tendency to let his mind wander from the action. A habit probably brought on by long spells of inactivity behind the curtain.

His friend, team-mate and admirer Willie Woodburn enjoys recalling the story of a game during a close-season tour in Denmark where a long-range shot which Bobby seemed to have covered inexplicably ended up in the net. 'For God's sake Bobby, what were you thinking about there?' roared Woodburn. Back came the answer: 'To tell you the truth, Ben, I was thinking about my garden at home'.

Woodburn will tell you Brown was a fine goalkeeper 'who put up the shutters for us often enough'.

However, Bobby's days at Ibrox were numbered after a disastrous opening League Cup tie against Hearts at Tynecastle on August 9, 1952. The blame for the 5-0 defeat was laid squarely on the goalkeeper, who still gets irked when inevitably in conversations that is the ONE match which people remember.

And it was at this moment he believes his part-time commitment was unfairly used against him.

'The boss Bill Struth called me in after the Hearts game and told me unless I could give him an assurance I would go full-time, then I would be out of the team to face Motherwell in midweek.'

'I didn't, and I was dropped. I felt my part-time role hadn't made any difference up to that point, and besides which players like Willie Waddell and Jock Shaw were running newsagents' shops and George Young had a hotel'.

But that was the beginning of the end for Bobby, although it was four years later before he departed through the famous swing doors of Ibrox. He made only one League Cup appearance in the season he was dropped, was back for twenty-one matches the following term but had by now lost out to George Niven.

He played only eleven times in the next two seasons and his last appearance was against East Fife on January 21, 1956 in the 3-0 win over East Fife.

Bobby was transferred to Falkirk for £2,200 in May 1956, but found that after Ibrox his heart was no longer in the game as a player and he was happy to quit football within a year.

That was the end of Bobby Brown, goalkeeper. But not the end of Bobby Brown and football. While teaching P.E. at Alloa Academy, he was offered the part-time post of manager to struggling St. Johnstone who were in the Second Division and desperate to restore the club's fortunes.

'I was keen to try the challenge, and it dovetailed nicely with my school job,' says Bobby. Within two years he had taken Saints to the Second Division championship and crowds had trebled to around the 10,000 mark.

It was then, for the first time in his life, that Bobby went full-time in football . . . . as manager/secretary at Muirton. This meant a move to the beautiful Perthshire village of Stanley. No hardship to a man whose biggest hobby was fishing, since there was a river at the foot of his garden.

'It was also a lovely spot for my wife Ruth and I to bring up our three daughters,' says Bobby.

He turned down the chance of managing Hibs in 1961, having decided to honour a new five-year contract with Saints. But he couldn't say no to his next invitation — to become Scotland's international team manager.

This was in 1966 after another ex-Rangers man, John Prentice, left the Scotland post following a short stay at Park Gardens.

'This was another tremendous challenge. And although I didn't enjoy ALL the next four years, it was a wonderful experience and brought me into contact with the best in football all over the world.'

'If I have any regrets, it's just that the system seemed to be stacked against you and also some players disappointingly never showed their club form in a Scotland jersey.'

Bobby's Scotland career got off to a memorable start, when the Jim Baxter-inspired side of 1967 defeated new World Cup holders England 3-2 at Wembley on April 15.

'That was a hard one to top,' says Bobby ruefully. Naturally it couldn't be done and Bobby found the frustrations of the job hard to take.

'The system has never changed. You can still find all your plans shattered by Saturday night withdrawals. It's hard to plan in the long term if this is going to be allowed to happen.'

'Happily I believe there is a lot more awareness now and co-operation from the clubs before big international games. But there will still be a lot of mysterious injuries cropping up.'

'Andy Roxburgh has a young and enthusiastic squad, and I believe he could do well if the will to help was truly there.'

Bobby's term of manager of Scotland lasted for four years in which time the team played twenty-eight games, won nine, drew eight and lost eleven.

'There were occasions when I had as many as nine withdrawals from a squad,' says Bobby wistfully.

'But I always got 100 per cent from John Greig, and big Alan Gilzean worked his heart out.'

Bobby's biggest disappointment was losing out in the World Cup qualifying game against West Germany in Hamburg in October 1969.

Two men who faced the problems of managing Scotland — Bobby Brown with the late Jock Stein.

'Gilzean got us back in the game at 2-2 in the second half and we were outplaying the Germans and looked likely to score.'

But then in a break after a fine save by Sepp Maier from John Greig, big Tommy Gemmell was caught too far upfield and that let Libuda through. We still had a chance to stop him, but our keeper Jim Herriott made a fatal hesitation and that was that'.

Bobby was dismissed from the Scotland job in 1971 .... and promptly set about building another new career as gift-shop owner and restaurateur in Helensburgh.

He spent six months training at a culinary course in Clydebank — 'the only man in a class of 18 women,' he recalls — and served in his restaurant in the evenings for many years until he decided enough was enough.

Sadly he lost his wife Ruth a few years ago after this coura-
geous lady had not only fought a long battle against bone
cancer, but also managed to raise thousands of pounds for
charity at the same time.

Still a trim, athletic figure, Bobby looks far too young for a
free bus pass — which is why he is the owner of a £300 hill bike,
loves long hill walks, swims and is an enthusiastic and
knowledgeable fisherman. Plus an indulgent grandfather
to his five grandchildren who live as far apart as Ayr and
Winchester.

INTERNATIONAL RECORD

Wartime internationals

1945

February 3 v.	England	(Villa Park)	2-3
April 14 v.	England	(Hampden)	1-6
November 12 v.	Wales	(Hampden)	2-0

1946

January 23 v.	Belgium	(Hampden)	2-2
February 2 v.	N. Ireland	(Belfast)	3-2
April 13 v.	England	(Hampden)	1-0
May 15 v.	Switzerland	(Hampden)	3-1

Full internationals

1946

November 27 v.	N. Ireland	(Hampden)	0-0

1948

November 17 v.	N. Ireland	(Hampden)	3-2

1952

April 5 v.	England	(Hampden)	1-2

League internationals

v. English League — 1949, 50, 51, 52
v. Irish League — 1951, 52
v. League of Ireland — 1951, 52

CHAPTER THREE

Eric Caldow

When the Scottish Football Association decided to form an exclusive over-50 club — with caps counting, not years — the news brought a wry smile to the face of Eric Caldow.

For there is no doubt that the former fleet-footed Rangers full back would have been a well-deserved member of that club . . . but for one reckless challenge that ended a glittering international career.

Eric Caldow heads for the 1962 Cup Final celebrations at Glasgow's St Enoch's Hotel.

The Caldow calamity came at Wembley, at six minutes past three on Saturday, April 6, 1963.

Eric was just 28. Captain of Scotland. Playing in his 18th consecutive international, and in his 40th game for his country.

George Young's proud record of being Rangers' most-capped player with 55 caps was well within Caldow's reach

But the fierce tackle by England's heavyweight striker Bobby Smith shattered not only that dream, but Caldow's leg in three places.

Eric still recalls the moment with painful clarity.

'I had cleared the ball away with my right foot, when Smith came flying in and caught my left leg. The ball must have been about six feet away by the time he hit me.'

'I knew I was in trouble right away, but of course didn't know the extent of the damage. I even managed a wee joke with the stretcher men as they carried me off.'

'At the time, I didn't put any blame on Smith for the accident. But what I didn't find out till a lot later was that Smith had told Denis Law BEFORE the game that Scotland would finish with ten men.'

'I still don't believe any professional footballer would set out to seriously injure another pro, but I must say my thoughts about Smith have never been kindly since.'

'Even the then Tottenham manager Bill Nicholson was appalled by the tackle by one of his own players, and Smith's career with Spurs didn't last much longer.'

Caldow's own career at international level was finished. And although he was back playing with Rangers reserves within six months, he was able to play only three League games for the first team in season 1963-64.

The following year proved to be Eric's last real go at the big time with Rangers. He played in 35 matches, including 26 League games and five European Cup ties.

But he was part of a team that was beginning to break up. The highly successful set-up that Scot Symon had brought together towards the end of the 1950s and into the 1960s was disintegrating.

Eric shows off the Scottish Cup at Hampden.

Caldow's injury was a factor. But then the other stars of the side began to depart the scene: Ian McMillan went back to Airdrie; Bobby Shearer was given a free at the end of the season; Jim Baxter was transferred to Sunderland; and Ralph Brand was off to Manchester City.

Eric's last full season was an ordinary one by Rangers' standards. They trailed fifth in the League and were knocked out of the Scottish Cup by Hibs in the third round.

But they had the consolation of a fine European Cup run which brought victories over Red Star Belgrade, after three games which climaxed in a play-off at Highbury; and then Rapid Vienna before they were eliminated in the quarter-finals by Inter Milan.

Above all, there was one high moment which Caldow surely deserved . . . victory over Celtic at Hampden in the League Cup Final.

'It was my third League Cup medal, and probably the one I treasure most', says Eric. 'It was the last major honour I won, and it climaxed for me a long hard fight back to fitness.'

'I must say that I thought I had recovered form well enough to be back in the Scotland team as well, but it wasn't to be.'

Eric's last Hampden appearance for Rangers was in a team captained by Jim Baxter, who orchestrated the 2-1 win over Celtic.

Jim Forrest scored two goals in ten minutes in the second half to set up the win, although Jimmy Johnstone got one back for Celtic with twenty minutes to go.

'I can also remember that before we got our second goal Celtic were furious with referee Hugh Phillips for turning down their appeals for an equaliser.'

'They were adamant that a shot from Bobby Murdoch which had squirmed out of Billy Ritchie's hands had gone over the line before he retrieved it. But the referee was having none of it.'

The teams in Eric's farewell appearance at Hampden on October 24, 1964 were:

Rangers: Ritchie, Provan, Caldow; Greig, McKinnon, Wood; Brand, Millar, Forrest, Baxter, Johnston.

Celtic: Fallon; Young, Gemmell; Clark, Cushley, Kennedy; Johnstone, Murdoch, Chalmers, Divers, Hughes.

That was the end of the Ibrox glory days for Eric. Let's go back to the beginning.

It was schoolteacher and local councillor Alex Sloan of Cronberry, just outside Cumnock, who first spotted the potential of the young Caldow.

'I think he was very friendly with the then Rangers director George Brown,' says Eric. 'I was playing with local youth sides like Glenpark and Townhead Thistle when I was signed for Rangers as a 14-year-old.'

'They farmed me out to Muirkirk Juniors for a spell before I was called up in 1952.'

That call-up caused quite a stir in the Caldow family.

'I had five brothers as well as two sisters', says Eric. 'And everyone of my brothers was a critic!'

'They came to watch me in every game, and my ears were ringing with criticism and advice after every match. One of them even turned down the chance of a trial with Muirkirk Juniors himself to carry on watching me.'

It was Bill Struth who signed Caldow, and even to this day the respect Eric felt for this great Rangers manager is still evident.

'He was a gentleman. He treated us as though we were all his family — yet at the same time you just KNEW not to get on the wrong side of him.'

'He was an amazing man. The first time he clapped his eyes on me, I was just a wee boy. But he told my father what height and weight I would grow to reach — and he was dead right.'

Caldow counts himself lucky to have been at Ibrox at a time when he was part of TWO great Rangers teams.

'The legendary 'Iron Curtain' side was just beginning to break up when I went to Rangers', says Eric.

'But the giants of football were still there. When I made my debut in a League Cup tie against Ayr United it was in place of George Young at right back. He was injured.'

'But I couldn't believe it when I looked around me at the men I was playing with: Ian McColl, Willie Woodburn, Sammy

Cox, Willie Waddell . . . it was unbelievable.'

'You can imagine how a teenager like myself felt. I've never felt so proud in all my life.'

Rangers won that quarter-final tie 4-2 at Ibrox, with John Prentice scoring a hat-trick. The teams are worth recording:

Rangers: Niven; Caldow, Little; McColl, Woodburn, Cox; Waddell, Grierson, Paton, Prentice, Hubbard.

Ayr United: Round; Rodger, Leckie; W. Fraser, McNeill, Cairns; Japp, Finnie, J. Fraser, Hutton, McKenna.

A crowd of 30,000 saw the young Caldow's debut that Saturday, September 12, 1953.

Altogether the teenage Caldow made 14 first-team appearances that season . . . one of them eminently forgettable.

Rangers were drawn against Aberdeen in the Scottish Cup semi-final, and were confidently expected to proceed to the Final.

What they got instead was a 6-0 drubbing, with Dons scoring four times in the last twenty minutes.

'I can just recall that I was up against a great wee winger in Jackie Hather and that Joe O'Neill scored a hat-trick for Aberdeen', says Eric. 'I think he was just back from a fractured skull, too.'

That was Bill Struth's last season in control at Ibrox. His replacement, Scot Symon, was a former Rangers player recruited from Preston after managing Dundee for a while.

And although Symon made Caldow his captain, and the team had great success, he is not a manager Eric recalls with any great fondness.

'I found him to be very rude at times, always aloof and capable of doing some cruel things to players. He never got close to the players, and the family atmosphere at Ibrox died away.'

'He set out to get rid of all Bill Struth's signings . . . and he did.'

'I recall that big George Young at the end of his career wanted to have a new two-year contract but would concentrate on playing with the reserves and bringing on the youngsters.'

'Symon told George that the directors had decided against this. But later we learned he had never put it to them.'

On parade: Caldow and team-mates Davie Wilson and Billy Ritchie show off the trophy at Hampden.

Eric himself felt badly treated some years later when during the Rangers tour of Russia in 1962 he and four other players opted for a visit to the British Embassy for 'a decent bit of food and a beer' instead of attending yet another after-match dinner with the Russians.

'Scot Symon didn't say anything to me at the time, but when we lined up for the official team photograph at the start of next season, he simply handed the ball over to Bobby Shearer.'

'That was the first moment I knew I was no longer captain. I was very disappointed, but by this time I knew that was the kind of thing the manager was capable of doing.'

Caldow's critical view of his boss extends into match tactics and his handling of the mercurial Jim Baxter.

'Scot wasn't very tactically aware. Basically he just urged us to give 100 per cent effort. We laid our own plans mostly, talking over the game on the bus on the way to away matches.'

Eric also believes that manager Symon was too soft with the wayward Jim Baxter.

'He got away with things no other player would have contemplated', says Eric.

'Such a brilliant player, too. I believe Symon did him no favours by overlooking misdemeanours.'

'If he had disciplined Jim the way the rest of us were, then I think Jim's career would have lasted a lot longer.'

Yet despite Eric's viewpoint, there is no denying that the Symon years were trophy-rich for Rangers. And Caldow shared in them.

'Yes, they were great. And my view of the manager is just a personal thing.'

'Being a Rangers player, captain of the club and of Scotland, brought me the kind of career and lifestyle I wouldn't have swopped for anything else.'

'Down in England, there was the £20 maximum wage. But at Rangers, with winning bonuses I could be earning up to £3,000 a year.'

'In fact, at one point when I was writing a guest column for the old *Sun* newspaper, I was getting £60 a week for that . . . which took me into the surtax bracket like a film star.'

'Miners in my home town of Cumnock were only getting about £7 a week, so you can see I was doing pretty well.'

And not just financially. In a playing sense, Caldow was one of the leading players in Europe.

Speed was his trademark. Caldow was reckoned to be the fastest full back in the world.

And that's not my view — it was expressed to Eric personally by the great Spanish winger Gento, the whirlwind star of the Real Madrid side of the 50s and 60s.

'I played against him a few times, and matched him for pace. He told me I was the fastest full back in the world.'

'He was certainly the best winger I ever encountered. The nearest we had in this country was wee Willie Henderson.'

'I thought Willie was a far better player, a more profitable winger than Jimmy Johnstone of Celtic, who was a great player as well. But Willie had the edge.'

Caldow's pace, and ability to play with equal ease on either side of the pitch, brought him his first full Scotland cap on April 6, 1957 . . . against England at Wembley.

It was a losing debut . . . Kevan and Edward scoring for England in a 2-1 win, with Tommy Ring getting the Scotland goal.

The young Rangers man obviously did enough to impress . . . he was kept on at right back for the next four internationals.

Then when Alex Parker was brought in at right back the versatile Caldow promptly switched to the left.

That was a facility Scotland was to appreciate time and again as Eric switched flanks readily to accommodate incoming players, left or right, like John Grant, Duncan McKay, John Hewie, club-mate Bobby Shearer and Alex Hamilton of Dundee.

'It didn't matter to me who I played with — or against,' says Eric.

'There was never a winger I didn't feel capable of catching, even if they got past me and had a good start.'

'My game was all about jockeying wingers, keeping tight on them until I got the chance to take the ball away.'

'Too many defenders nowadays play on their backsides — they are sliding in at the first go. I never believed in that.'

'Mind you, the way the game is played nowadays, with hardly any wingers, I would be still playing at 50. In my time, you had enough trouble looking after your winger without making too many runs upfield.'

'The likes of Kurt Hamrin the Swedish winger with Fiorentina and Gento wouldn't have stood back and let a full back go on the attack. They would have been after you like a shot — and if you were caught too far upfield with the pace these guys had, you would never get near them again.'

Caldow's own speed was obviously natural. But it was also certainly latent when he was a boy.

'I was the slowest schoolboy in Cumnock', he declares. 'I couldn't win a race to save myself.'

'But then when I was 15 I went on to spikes — and within months had gained yards. I would recommend spikes for any young player. Indeed, I trained for the rest of my football life with them.'

Eric's first taste of the success that was to fill his career came in season 1955-56, Scot Symon's second full season in charge at Ibrox.

Major changes had been made in the side in the time Symon was in charge. Players like Jimmy Millar (Dunfermline), Max Murray (Queen's Park) and Sammy Baird (Preston) were all recruited. And a bustling big centre forward from South Africa was signed . . . Don Kichenbrand, quickly nicknamed 'The Rhino' and a man who made his mark — literally! — on Scottish football.

With the *sine die* suspension of Willie Woodburn Rangers had switched George Young to centre-half. And the young Caldow was given the task of filling the giant boots of 'Corky'.

'That wasn't easy. He was the greatest Rangers player of all as far as I'm concerned', says Eric.

Eric's full-back partner was Johnny Little for the first part of the season. But in December Rangers signed the fiery red-haired Bobby Shearer from Hamilton Accies for £2,000.

And by January 1956 he and Caldow were teamed up to form a partnership that helped bring honour after honour to the Ibrox club.

'We called Bobby 'Captain Cutlass' for good reason', says Eric. 'What a fierce competitor he was. He gave everything for Rangers, but boy was he hard on some wingers.'

Eric recalls fondly that Shearer's ferocity in one instance was extended to take in a substitute.

'It was during a summer tour of Spain in 1956 and we went to Minorca to play. Nobody had even heard of Minorca at that time.'

'We played in the capital Mahon on a sand pitch. During the game a pass meant for their left winger was going off the pitch and one of their subs was foolish enough to get off the bench and put his foot out to stop it going too far over the line.'

'Bobby was in full pursuit, and he didn't bother to draw back. He got to the ball at the same time as the substitute and promptly booted the ball and the Spaniard at the same time. The fellow had to be taken away on a stretcher . . . and he wasn't even on the pitch!'

Rangers won the League in '55-56 by six points with the defence conceding only 27 goals in 34 games . . . compared with the 50 lost by second-placed Aberdeen.

Caldow played in all but eight of the League matches and picked up the first of his FIVE championship medals.

That flag win took Rangers into the newly-devised European Cup for the first time.

It was a brief, battling, sometimes bizarre excursion.

Rangers were drawn against French champions Nice.

'European football meant nothing to us at that point', says Eric. 'No one realised the significance of the event . . . or could visualise how it would turn into the most important football development of all time in Europe.'

'I mean, no-one went to see the opposition play. They just turned up and we took them on.'

A crowd of 65,000 turned up at Ibrox on October 24, 1956 for their first game with Nice. They saw Rangers hit back after losing a first-half goal to win 2-1. What they didn't see was a piece of dressing-room comedy.

'When the English referee Arthur Ellis blew for full-time I was off the pitch in a flash,' says Eric. 'I had been best man at my brother's wedding and was heading back for the reception.'

'I had my gear off and was ready to drop in the bath when big George Young came in and told me we had to go back on the pitch — the referee had blown about six minutes early.'

In the return leg, Nice won 2-1 in a match that sizzled despite a downpour. Ibrox wing-half Billy Logie was ordered off after being punched in the face by Nice striker Bravo.

'Billy never got a chance to retaliate, but he was certainly intending to get some revenge', recalls Caldow. The game was actually two weeks late — having already been postponed once because of a waterlogged pitch.

There were no penalty shoot-outs in those days, so two weeks later Rangers were in Paris for a play-off which they lost 3-1.

Rangers were back in Europe the following season after winning the League again . . . the club's 30th flag success. But they had to fight all the way for the title.

'I can recall we were behind Hearts for most of the season, and had to put in a strong finish to pip them by a couple of points', says Eric.

It was also the season when Eric's international career took off. He had won Under-23 honours against England when he was picked for the Scottish League against the English League at Ibrox on March 13, 1957 . . . and played his part in a 3-2 victory.

That was the first of 14 League honours for Eric and his full international debut came less than a month later.

Caldow's career was launched, and he was in victorious sides against Spain (4-2 at Hampden), Switzerland (2-1 in Basle) and West Germany (3-1 in Stuttgart) before the winning run was halted in Madrid when Spain beat Scotland 4-1.

Not that Eric remembered much about that World Cup qualifying defeat.

'I collided with our goalkeeper Tommy Younger after 25 minutes', says Eric.

'I must have been concussed for I don't recall any other part of the game. And I played all through it!'

In those early Scotland days, as at Ibrox, big George Young was the dominant figure.

'He was captain, and team manager', says Eric. 'And he did a great job of it. But it was in that same game against Spain that the S.F.A. did the dirty on Corky.'

'He had announced after the game against Switzerland that the match against Spain, due the next week, would be his last. That seemed to get up the noses of the selectors — and they promptly dropped him.'

'George was in tears. I felt like joining him. What petty minds were at work then to do this to such a great player.'

Caldow went on to emulate his hero Young and captain

Swapping pennants: Caldow with Fiorentina captain Orzan before a European tie.

Scotland, and was still skipper when his career ended on that fateful Wembley afternoon.

He won 29 of his Scotland caps at left back and 11 at right back.

'Scotland had some great teams and great players in those

days . . . it makes you wonder why we didn't do better at times', says Eric. 'Probably we were not organised or prepared properly.'

Apart from being a full back with speed and class, Eric was also a penalty expert . . . although as he says himself he 'did miss a few'.

He scored four times for Scotland and during an average season with Rangers was good for potting about half a dozen.

With George Young gone, Rangers tried to find a suitable replacement in 1957-58. A search that was intensified after the stunning 7-1 defeat by Celtic in the League Cup at Hampden and led to seasoned campaigner Willie Telfer being pulled in from St. Mirren.

By the following season, Rangers had settled enough to take their 31st League title — courtesy of Celtic.

'We went into the final day of the season two points ahead of Hearts — and we lost at home against Aberdeen', recalls Eric. 'You can imagine how grateful we were to hear the news that Celtic had beaten Hearts at Parkhead.'

Eric maintains that he always had friendly relationships with the Celtic players, and quite often shared a pint with the Parkhead men.

'We always wanted to win the Old Firm game — and so did Celtic', says Eric. 'But the bitterness was confined to the terracings as far as most of us were concerned.'

Although Caldow remained with Rangers for a career span of fifteen seasons, he almost departed Ibrox in 1959.

Manchester United came in for him, and a then record fee for a full back was agreed — £47,000.

But the move never transpired . . . because of £2,000.

That was the going 'cut' for big transfers at the time — and was what Caldow asked for . . . but didn't get.

'The only reason I wanted to move was the lump sum', says Eric. 'I was on good earnings at Ibrox, but £2,000 would have bought your house in those days and it was given to Dave Mackay when he moved from Hearts to Spurs and Bobby Collins when he left Celtic for Everton.'

'So I wanted the same. But Matt Busby the United boss was having none of it. He refused to pay, and since the minimum wage was still in operation in England I knew I was better off staying with Rangers.'

That decision was to mean Eric earning his first Scottish Cup medal in the 2-0 defeat of Kilmarnock, despite Caldow missing a second-half penalty.

'I fairly blasted it high over the bar', says Eric. 'We were only leading 1-0 at the time and I was glad when Jimmy Millar headed in our second goal.'

Had Eric gone south, he would also have missed out on what was to be a vastly rewarding era which began for Rangers in 1960. It was then that Jim Baxter arrived at Ibrox, the final piece in the jig-saw which Scot Symon put together to form a picture team.

Between 1960 and 1965 when Baxter departed for Sunderland, Rangers won three League championships; four Scottish Cups, including three in a row from 1962; and three League Cups. They also reached the Final of the 1961 Cup Winners Cup where they lost to Fiorentina over two legs.

'It was certainly a tremendous spell. But it wasn't all due to Jim Baxter', says Eric.

'Ranges won trophies before and after Jim.'

'But there is no doubt that he was brilliant. He could just about make the ball talk with that left foot.'

'However, it was the blend of that team that was right. We had brilliance in Baxter and McMillan, strength in Shearer and Davis and speed in other areas.'

'I used to have to do all Baxter's defensive work for him. There was no way he could mark a fast player. But I didn't mind. It was for the team.'

The success at home never brought the European medal which Caldow and the other Rangers men of that time would have liked.

'At one time I didn't think a British team could do it. But Celtic proved me wrong — and opened up the way for the others,' says Eric.

He has a few good memories of European games . . . like the trip to Wolverhampton when 10,000 Rangers supporters marched through the town to the ground to cheer the Ibrox men to success against what was regarded as the best in England.

'I'll never forget it. I was lying on my bed in the hotel relaxing on the afternoon of the match when this tremendous volume of noise rocked the place. I couldn't believe it when I looked out the window and saw all those fans marching and singing 'Follow Follow'.'

'We knew we had to win through for them that night. And we did.'

Huge crowds abounded for big matches. There were 126,930 at Hampden for the 1962 Scottish Cup Final which Rangers won 2-0 against St. Mirren; earlier 57,000 had watched a replay against Aberdeen at Ibrox.

By contrast they also played before the smallest crowd ever — or since — for a European tie. Only 1,781 were in the stadium at Malmo in Sweden as Rangers played a 'home' tie against Vorwaerts of East Germany who had been refused permits to enter Britain.

The game was played at 9 a.m. on a wet Thursday morning, which might explain the attendance!

Recalls Eric: 'The tie actually went on the previous night, but had to be abandoned at half-time because of fog. It was an eerie experience playing a European tie at breakfast time. Luckily we won through easily on aggregate.'

Rangers took the championship by nine clear points from Kilmarnock in 1962-63, a season when only two League games were lost.

But because of the Arctic conditions which hit Scotland that year, there were still 13 games of the 34-match programme to go when Caldow's calamity at Wembley happened. So he was a spectator for the months of April and May as first the flag and then the Scottish Cup went to Ibrox, with Celtic being beaten 3-0 in the Final replay at Hampden.

His time at Ibrox ran out in April 1966, when he was given a free transfer.

In 13 seasons he played in 464 games of all kinds for Rangers, including 265 League matches.

Wembley agony for Caldow, and the end of his international career, April 6, 1963.

AND NOT ONCE IN ALL THOSE YEARS WAS HE BOOKED.

'I never felt the need to kick anyone', says Eric. 'I was blessed with a very placid temperament.'

Eric was tempted into the management side of football for a time, first of all as player-boss of English non-league club Corby and then with Stranraer.

But he found, like so many others, that working with directors was a difficult proposition.

'Corby won three Cups in my first season with them. But then I asked for permission from the chairman to go up north to be interviewed for the job as manager of Raith Rovers — Jimmy Millar got the post as it happens — and this was agreed.'

'Our game was off at the weekend, anyway. But when I came back I was called in and told the board had decided to fire me!'

Then at Stranraer, after taking them on such a good League run that the club collected £16,000 in points money from the League's pools pay-out, he asked the club for £4,000 to buy big striker Neil Hood from Hamilton Accies.

'The next thing I knew was that, despite having signed a new contract just before Christmas, I was phoned just after New Year and told I would have to go because of economy cuts.'

'Big John Hughes of Celtic got the job after me, spent £10,000 on team building — and then he was sacked, too.'

That was enough to convince Caldow to make his living outside football. He ran a couple of pubs for a while, but is currently back on the road as Scottish representative for Keith Young Insulation.

He and wife Laura are grandparents now, with daughter Jacquie married to a policeman in Dalmellington, not far from the Caldow home in Mauchline, and son Eric is now based in Manchester.

Golf, and weekends spent caravanning are Eric's interests. But he likes to see Rangers when he can and is a great admirer of the job being done by Graeme Souness in transforming the Ibrox team.

'He has revolutionised Scottish football. Everyone has benefited', says Caldow. 'And I believe if he gets on with the job the way he wants Rangers will have a fantastic team in the future.'

Eric's only complaints are the lack of entertainment in too many games; the stupidity of players getting booked or ordered off for dissent . . . and the hasty way too many referees are ready to produce the yellow or red card.

'Our refs don't seem to be able to have a bit of chit-chat with the players the way they can in England. It would improve our game if they were more flexible.'

INTERNATIONAL RECORD

1957

Apr.	England	(a)	1-2
May	Spain	(h)	4-2
May	Switzerland	(a)	2-1
May	W. Germany	(a)	3-1
May	Spain	(a)	1-4
Oct.	N. Ireland	(a)	1-1
Nov.	Switzerland	(h)	3-2
Nov.	Wales	(h)	1-1

1958

May	Hungary	(h)	1-1
June	Poland	(a)	2-1
June	Yugoslavia	(WC, Sweden)	1-1
June	France	(WC)	1-2
June	Paraguay	(WC)	2-3
Oct.	Wales	(a)	3-0
Oct.	N. Ireland	(h)	2-2

1959

Apr.	England	(a)	0-1
May	W. Germany	(h)	3-2
May	Holland	(a)	2-1
May	Portugal	(a)	0-1
Oct.	N. Ireland	(a)	4-0
Nov.	Wales	(h)	1-1

1960

Apr.	England	(h)	1-1
May	Austria	(a)	1-4
June	Hungary	(a)	3-3
June	Turkey	(a)	2-4
Oct.	Wales	(a)	0-2
Nov.	N. Ireland	(h)	5-2

1961

Apr.	England	(a)	3-9
May	Eire	(h)	4-1
May	Eire	(a)	3-0
May	Czechoslovakia	(a)	0-4
Sept.	Czechoslovakia	(h)	3-2
Oct.	N. Ireland	(a)	6-1
Nov.	Wales	(h)	2-0
Nov.	Czechoslovakia		2-4
		(play-off, Brussels)	

1962

Apr.	England	(h)	2-0
May	Uruguay	(h)	2-3
Oct.	Wales	(a)	3-2
Nov.	N. Ireland	(h)	5-1

1963

Apr.	England	(a)	2-1

Caldow also won 14 inter-League caps and two Under-23 honours.

CHAPTER FOUR

Ralph Brand

There must be hundreds of people who have studied the face of the taxi driver who has picked them up in one of Edinburgh's busy steets and said: 'I know him — but from where?'

Many would opt for boxing, for Ralph Brand's features carry the battered look of a successful (well sometimes) light middleweight.

But it was with his feet, not his hands, that Brand became famous. Not that you would know it from his demeanour. Nor would he volunteer the information too readily.

Ralph Brand always has been, and remains, a private, intense person.

As a player Ralph put so much into a match he was 'shattered' and often took nearly an hour to bath and change.

'I'm not surprised,' says his former Ibrox colleague Ian

In for the kill — but this time Ralph Brand shoots over the bar against Queen of the South, George Farm defending.

McMillan. 'He ran so hard and long I was always amazed. And yet at the end of it all, Ralph was always the one guy who wanted to probe deeply into the whys and wherefores of a game.'

He found few to have such conversations with — most of the players were out of the bath and out of the door before Ralph had his boots off.

'I always found that frustrating,' says Ralph. 'I wanted to sit and talk over the game, try to analyse the play. We didn't seem to THINK too much about what had happened.'

Brand's dedication to the game of football goes right back to his primary school days at Murrayburn in the same Edinburgh district where he was born, bred and still lives.

'I can remember the head teacher asking my mother what I wanted to be when I grew up. Even at the age of eight she could tell him I was going to be a footballer. I don't think he believed her, thinking it was just the same as those kids who were going to be pilots or engine drivers.'

Where his footballing ambition came from he has no idea — since there were no other sports-minded members of the family, although Ralph says that his mother had a bit of a reputation as a runner in the days when there used to be sports days held in the various villages that made up the outlying districts of Edinburgh.

But he knows where he got his urge to become a Rangers player . . . . from a Glasgow-based uncle who used to visit the Brand household and regale the youngster with tales of players like Willie Woodburn, George Young, Willie Waddell and Willie Thornton.

Brand was hooked on Rangers from then on — but never expected to find himself training alongside those legends within a few years.

'When I went to secondary school at Carrickvale, I was too wee to get a game in the first team,' recalls Ralph. 'But I was determined to do it.'

A team-mate in those days was Ken Ross, who went on to become a Scotland rugby cap. And also at Carrickvale was Dave Mackay.

Ralph scores following a rebound in a match at Firhill against Partick Thistle.

Dave was of course a local hero — capped twice as a school-boy for Scotland, then on to Hearts, Tottenham and inter-national fame.

Ralph Brand traced his footsteps — part of the way.

The then 15-year-old Ralph became the first 'star' to be dis-covered via television. He played for Scotland schools in the game against England at Wembley in 1952. The game was on the box for the first time and the boy Brand impressed a lot of viewers — including Rangers manager Bill Struth.

A few of Ralph's team-mates in those schoolboys days also went on to senior fame . . . goalkeeper Chic Brodie, centre half Doug Baillie, winger Johnny Lawlor. Also in the squad were Adam Blacklaw, Billy Reid and Jackie Plenderleith.

The result of Ralph's TV ratings was a visit from Rangers scout Bob Macauley . . . . followed later by a telegram from Bill Struth.

'You can imagine the excitement that caused in the house,' says Ralph. 'The telegram told me to phone Mr Struth at Ibrox at a certain time.'

'I made the call from the coin box at the corner of Sighthill Road — the first time I had ever used the phone, I think.'

That phone call took Ralph through to Ibrox to meet the legendary Struth, and committed him to join Rangers at the appropriate time as a full-time player.

Before then Ralph played for Slateford Athletic, then farmed out to junior club Broxburn to gain experience. While with Broxburn he broke his wrist, and there are many of that club's supporters who still believe that his injury cost them the chance of Junior Cup glory.

His debut for Rangers reserves against Ayr United as a 16-year-old ended with him in hospital — he got concussion in a mid-air collision and was detained in the Victoria Infirmary overnight.

Ralph's introduction to the top team came two years later, on November 6, 1954, against Kilmarnock at Ibrox. This time there was no injury — just the first signs of a scoring habit that was to stay with him throughout his career.

Rangers won 6-0, with Brand scoring the second and last of the goals, playing on the right wing in place of the injured Willie Waddell.

It's worth recording the side in which the teenager received his baptism:
Niven; Little, Cox; McColl, Young, Rae; Brand, Paton, Simpson, Grierson, Hubbard.

He played the following week against Falkirk at Brockville, didn't score but the team won 3-0.

Then on December 4 he played his third — and last — League game of that season.

Says Ralph: 'It was against Q.o.S. at Palmerston on a terrible day, with driving freezing rain.'

'I was so wee and light that by the end of the game the shoulders of my shirt were down at my elbows. I must have looked pitiful.'

Brand bullets in a header against Hibs.

The upshot was a bout of pneumonia which put the stripling Brand out of action for many weeks.

He did recover in time to play one Scottish Cup tie — the 0-0 draw with Dundee at Ibrox, but was missing when Rangers won the replay 1-0.

Ralph recalls those early days with considerable relish. 'I would travel through to Ibrox for training by bus when I was a part-timer,' he says. 'It was the only way I knew how to get to Glasgow, following the route we took as a family when going to visit my relatives.'

'Bill Struth was like a grandfather to the young players. He was kindly, but you knew you had to be smart and respectful or else.'

'I found that out early on. I was making a good few bob for a youngster, and fancied myself as a trendy young buck. So one day I went into Alexander the Tailors in Edinburgh and bought myself what I thought was a smart jacket — herringbone, made to measure with a shawl collar and four patch pockets.'

'There were royal blue serge trousers with no turn-ups, and just a bit on the narrow side in the fashion of the day.'

'I'll never know yet how the boss managed to see me arriving. Maybe he was at the window of his flat near the ground when I came off the subway. Maybe he saw me from his office. Or maybe someone told him.'

'Anyway I was hardly through the door when the doorman told me I was wanted upstairs. I was quaking when I went up the marble steps. Young though I was I knew you were SUMMONED up there, you just didn't wander.'

On the door to the manager's office, and still there, is a buzzer which visitors press — and then a light comes on illuminating the words 'wait' in red, or 'enter' in green.

'I don't think ANYONE got the green light straight away,' says Ralph. 'That was Bill Struth psychology at work.'

'Anyway when I got in he was sitting there at that huge desk of his, with his walking stick perched on top of the glass. It must have been reinforced stuff, for he suddenly picked up his stick and walloped the table with an almighty crack.'

'I went about five feet up in the air, and I'm sure I must have nearly changed the colour of those blue trousers.'

Struth thundered: 'You are a Rangers player. We pay you good money. Don't ever come to Ibrox dressed like that again. Go home and change.'

Watched by an anxious Celtic goalkeeper Frank Haffey, Brand heads wide at Hampden.

And that's just what Ralph had to do — all the way back to Edinburgh and back again in the late afternoon. However, as he recalls, Struth showed another of those subtle touches by telling Brand to go to the club tailors and get fitted out with the official club blazer and slacks — which normally were given only to players who toured with the club.

National Service took Brand out of the Ibrox scene for the next two seasons, but a disastrous League start to season 1957-58, followed by the League Cup Final against Celtic at Hampden which ended in the stunning 7-1 defeat, made it clear to Rangers, now bossed by Scot Symon, that it was time to reshape the side.

Brand came in to play in 22 League games and scored 11 times. He also netted three in the Scottish Cup.

That should have been Brand on his way, and it was . . . up to a point. He played 25 League games and scored 21 goals, including a hat trick against Q.o.S. (revenge for the pneumonia perhaps). That made him top League scorer, four ahead of Max Murray in a season where Rangers won the title for the 31st time.

'But I still felt that I was the one liable to be dropped out if things went wrong,' says Ralph.

And so it proved. He made only nine League appearances in '59-60, despite having opened the season in spectacular style with four goals against Hibs in a 6-1 League Cup triumph at Easter Road.

'I felt great after that game. But Scot Symon soon put my feet back on the ground. His only comment in the dressing room was: 'You didn't half miss a few out there.' I went home in tears instead of jubilation.'

'But it was then I decided that if I were to stay in that Rangers team, then the only thing that would keep me there was goals.'

'They couldn't keep me out if I kept on scoring. If I couldn't get a game on the wing, then it would be at inside forward. So I worked harder than ever on my speed and anticipation.'

'I was never above ten stone in all my playing days at Ibrox so I wasn't built for heavy work. I relied on my speed off the mark to do the job.'

But at the start of 1960-61, Ralph was in a seat in the stand watching a new boy make his mark at inside-left for Rangers . . . Jim Baxter, signed from Raith Rovers in the close season for £17,500.

'I thought I'd had it then,' says Ralph. 'But it was at this point it became clear that Scot Symon was putting together a team of tremendous ability.'

'I've always regretted that I never did sit down with him and find out how much was planned, how much just happened and how much was luck.'

'But he certainly got the blend right. Bobby Shearer and Eric Caldow were contrasting full backs, but so effective. Same with Bill Paterson at centre half. Harry Davis was a power in defence; Jim Baxter and Ian McMillan a wonderful pair in midfield and up front the balance of Willie Henderson or Alex Scott on the right, with Davie Wilson on the left and Jimmy Millar and myself going through the middle proved just right.'

'Right' is hardly the word for it. Rangers took the title for the 32nd time, beating Kilmarnock by a point. They also won the League Cup.

And in both these competitions, Brand was blistering. He played in all 34 League games, and finished top scorer with 24 goals. He netted nine more in the League Cup, including a hat-trick against Queen of the South again in the 7-0 semi-final victory at Parkhead, and the first goal in the 2-0 Final win over Kilmarnock at Hampden.

There was also a hat-trick for Brand in the 8-0 Ibrox thrashing of Borussia M.G. of Germany in the European Cup Winners Cup — a display that Ian McMillan reckons is one of the best Rangers have ever given.

The next few years were glory times for Rangers. And Brand. He finished top scorer again in '60-61 with 23 League strikes, 9 in the League Cup, 6 in the Scottish Cup . . . . a total of 42 in all games.

By this time a 'brace for Brand' was becoming a common quote in the newspaper match reports.

'There used to be a newsvendor at Queen Street station who used to ask me after every game, not IF I had scored but HOW MANY,' recalls Ralph.

Two of his goals came in Hampden Finals — in the 3-1 win over Hearts in the League Cup and 2-0 victory over St. Mirren in the Scottish.

Indeed, in his Ibrox career Brand played in seven major Finals for Rangers at Hampden, was never on a losing side and scored six goals.

He carried his striking performances into the international scene as well.

In eight full internationals, he scored eight times. In five League Internationals he also netted eight goals, including four against the hapless Irish League in a 7-0 win at Ibrox on October 3, 1961.

Yet despite this glut of goals, Brand never seemed to find acceptance with selectors or spectators.

He still finds this ironical.

'The fans used to shout that I was nothing but a poacher. In fact, I got that in one game against Aberdeen at Pittodrie when I broke from my own half of the field and scored a great goal,' laughs Ralph.

'And in the international scene, well Denis Law was very much the man, wasn't he.'

Ralph scored the Scottish League's goal in the 1-1 draw with the Italian League at Hampden in November 1961 — and was booed off the park because he had missed a number of chances.

Ralph's answer was to work even harder.

'I used to talk Jimmy Millar and David Wilson into coming back in the afternoons so that we could practise working at close-passing moves,' says Ralph. 'It used to drive Scot Symon potty — 'don't play it so tight' he would tell us.'

'But long before we realised it we were playing 4-2-4, with myself lying between the opposition half-backs and the centre half ready to link up with Jimmy Millar through the middle.'

Ralph also recalls another move which drove manager Symon to depair — the wearing of lightweight boots which Brand and Ian McMillan picked up in Italy after a game against Milan.

'The boss said we would be crippled by the opposition, and even went as far as designing and having manufactured his own boots — the JSS model. But it didn't stop me. Speed was what I needed. And good control. So I was willing to take a chance that the skinlifters would get me.'

'Skinlifters', incidentally, is Ralph's now affectionate term for the harder-tackling members of his profession, although he didn't feel so kindly disposed to them when he was playing.

'I can remember playing as a boy against Bobby Parker of Hearts, and he seemed a fearsome figure. He told me at the start of the game: 'The next time you pass me on the outside,

Brand beats Hibs goalkeeper Wren to complete a hat-trick at Easter Road.

son, it will be on the other side of that wall', pointing to the boundary fence.'

'When I told Ian McColl this, he said: 'Just do to him what you do to us in training.' I did, and never had any bother with Bobby. He was just trying to intimidate me, I guess.'

By the mid-60s, Ralph's career with Rangers was reaching a critical stage.

'Like most players, I felt I was due more money. And I also felt the way we prepared for football, and our tactics, were not changing to meet the rising standards of elsewhere.'

'And when Jim Baxter went to Sunderland in May, 1965, I decided it was time for me to move on, too.'

Move he did, to Manchester City for £30,000 on August 10 1965. But it turned out to be a bitter parting.

'In my anger I said a lot of things for a series of newspaper articles which must have hurt Scot Symon deeply,' says Ralph.

'It was sheer frustration. And after the first of them was printed, I tried to get Manchester City manager Joe Mercer to have them stopped. But it couldn't be done.'

'It wasn't until after he himself had been sacked by Rangers and was with Partick Thistle that Scot seemed to forgive me.'

Brand's career in England never carried the same success. He left Manchester after a couple of years, to link up with Jim Baxter again at Sunderland.

By now he was a keen attender at the English F.A. coaching school, his imagination fired by the works of the legendary Malcolm Allison — 'the best coach I've ever seen.'

He came back to Scotland in 1969 to link up as a player-coach under old friend Jimmy Millar at Raith Rovers. Then came spells as coach/manager of Albion Rovers (twice), Darlington, before finally in 1975 he had to leave as coach of Dunfermline because of the club's economy cuts.

With a growing family of four, three sons and a daughter (who has now made him a grandfather), Ralph launched out in the taxi business in Edinburgh.

Which is where he still is — independent as ever. Reserved as ever. But with a post-war League scoring record of 127 goals in 203 games which helped his club win four titles, this truly qualifies him as one of Rangers' great forwards.

He still is intense about football, and aims to spread his knowledge to the younger generations through a series of coaching schools. And relaxes with a game of golf every week at Baberton.

Amazingly, the stammer which was with him all his playing days has more or less vanished.

'It was nerves, I guess,' he says. 'I was so uptight I couldn't have told you after a game what my direct opponent looked like. He could have been Frank Sinatra as far as I knew. The only thing I would notice was if he was hard to beat. If he was, I just tried even harder.'

INTERNATIONAL RECORD

FULL CAPS

1960			
November	N. Ireland	(Hampden)	5-2
1961			
May	Rep. of Ireland	(Hampden)	4-1
May	Rep. of Ireland	(Dublin)	3-0
May	Czechoslovakia	(Bratislava)	0-4
October	N. Ireland	(Belfast)	6-1
November	Wales	(Hampden)	2-0
November	Czechoslovakia	(Brussels)	2-4 (a.e.t.)
1962			
May	Uruguay	(Hampden)	2-3

CHAPTER FIVE

Ian McMillan

Ian McMillan doesn't mind being called a 'bum' player. Indeed he is amused by former team-mate Ralph Brand's description of Ian as 'one of the great bum players of all time.'

'That's typical of Ralph,' he says. 'He was always a shrewd observer of the game although not many people knew that at the time when he was playing.'

McMillan, the man they dubbed the 'Wee Prime Minister' in his short but highly successful career with Rangers, admits readily that his posterior was an important element in his playing style.

Ian McMillan shows the control that made him such a skilful player.

The start of a Russian
tour — McMillan with
youthful John Greig
to his right.

'I wasn't fast so I had to find other ways to keep myself clear
of tackles from defenders. I inherited a large backside from my
mother's side of the family so I decided to put it to good use.'

'When I got the ball, I immediately leaned forward, sticking
out my bum so that it was very hard for a defender to get too
close to me.'

Brand picks up the description from there.

'Ian would manoeuvre the guy trying to tackle him by simply turning the defender round to the far side from the ball by
using his bum. They just couldn't get near him. It must have
been helluva frustrating for them.'

McMillan was 27, already nearing the veteran stage in some
eyes, when Rangers stepped in to pay Airdrie £10,000 for him
in 1958.

His brother Hamish had already been a Rangers player, as had one of his cousins — and Ian's name had been linked with the Ibrox club several times during his eleven-year career with Airdrie.

'But it was still a surprise when it happened,' says Ian. 'I was in dispute with Airdrie at the time and hadn't played a game since the start of the season.'

'It was all about a bonus payment. In those days clubs could pay a loyalty payment of £250 to a player after five years' service. I had been due one after my first five years with the club, but asked them to delay it for a year or so because I was to be married and the money would be very handy at that time.'

'Then when the next five years were up, I asked for my next bonus and was astonished when the directors said I wasn't due it because I had received one only four years previously.'

'They just wouldn't accept the fact that I had delayed payment of the first bonus and was due the second. I will never understand why they did that after all the years of service I had given them.'

'At any rate, there was no agreement by the start of the season so I was playing golf on a Saturday afternoon instead of football.'

So the move to Rangers couldn't have come at a better time for Ian . . . . or for the Ibrox club.

Manager Scot Symon was at this time in the process of rebuilding. His team had strength and power in abundance. Now it needed subtlety. McMillan supplied it — but not right away.

He had to spend a couple of weeks in training before he was ready for action — but throughout his career with Rangers Supermac was always a part-timer, working as a quantity surveyor in Airdrie before ultimately setting up his own painting business.

When he did make his debut, it was against Raith Rovers . . . and against a young man playing at left half in the Kirkcaldy team who was later to become the second half of the most famous inside forward duo — they were not called midfield men in those days — yes, Jim Baxter.

Thanks pal! McMillan acknowledges help after scoring against Third Lanark.

There was no doubt who gained the advantage that day, October 18, 1958.

New man McMillan scored the first and last of the goals in a 4-0 victory at Ibrox. The teams that day were:
Rangers: Niven; Shearer, Little; McColl, Telfer, Davis; Duncan, McMillan, Scott, Baird, Hubbard.
Raith: Thorburn, Polland, Williamson; Ward, McNaught, Baxter; McEwan, Kerry, Dobbie, Young, Urquhart.

Rangers, with the Wee Prime Minister in residence at Ibrox, swept round the country. A run of twenty-seven games with only one defeat brought McMillan his first League Championship badge as the Glasgow side took the title by two points from Hearts, who knew the flag was unlikely to be theirs when they were thrashed 5-0 before a 60,000 crowd at Ibrox on December 13.

For Ian McMillan, the change from Airdrie to Rangers was hard to take in . . . . even though he had already won international honours, having won three caps in 1952 and also being included in the side that lost 7-2 to the English at Wembley in 1955.

'But at least that game let me see the magic of Stanley Matthews at close range,' recalls Ian. 'You know, he was 40 years old at the time. And he still left men nearly half his age for dead with pace and control. He devastated us — all we could do at the end of the game was add to the congratulations he deserved.'

It's here that McMillan, a respected player all his career with both his clubs, makes a confession: 'I never felt I was good enough to play at that very top level. I used to step on the pitch, look at players like Matthews and Billy Wright, and say to myself, 'What am I doing here?' '

'It's a matter of personal character of course. But I just wish I'd been given some of the natural arrogance which flowed so easily and so tellingly through the players like Jim Baxter and Willie Henderson.'

McMillan, of course, does himself an injustice. But a look at his background probably explains his inhibitions. He was and remains an Airdrieonian. Brought up in Adam Street, a good free kick from Broomfield where his father Jimmy was first of all head checker and ultimately secretary in a lifetime given to his cherished Airdrie.

Ian was destined to be a first-team player at the tender age of 17 — but not before serving time as a 'Brusher', which is the nickname given to all pupils of Albert Primary, and for a short spell playing with the local Drumpellier Amateurs.

'They were sponsored by McLarens the local undertakers — and the team strip was all black,' says Ian with some relish.

He made his first-team debut aged 17 against Cowdenbeath at Broomfield. And the *Sunday Mail* headline of the day said of the 3-1 victory: 'Boy Internationalist shines for Airdrie'. Ian was never a schoolboy cap, but he was soon a school hero at Airdrie Academy as he settled into the top team.

Read all about it! Ian learns of Billy Steel's injury and his own first international cap.

'Those were fun days,' recalls Ian. 'We had a skipper called Willie Kelly who used to smoke like a chimney in the toilet just before we went out. And his final words were always: 'right lads, same as last week.'

'It didn't matter that we might have been beaten 6-0 last week!'

Ian also recalls with pleasure the sight of Willie 'Cowboy' McCulloch, coming in off the left wing to have a pot at goal with his right foot.

'As soon as the shareholders on the balcony of the old pavilion saw this, they all ducked. Nine times out of ten a right-foot shot from Cowboy would rattle between the seats and the roof of the balcony!'

When the dispute finally made him leave Broomfield, the club built a new enclosure with his transfer fee and Ian still reckons the fans call it after him.

'Personally I didn't get a penny out of the £10,000 transfer deal,' says Ian. 'That's how naive I was. But since my part-time wages tripled to around £30, I probably was very pleased at the time.'

At Ibrox, Ian quickly discovered the one man he could communicate best with was the taciturn Fifer Harold Davis, a powerful physical presence in any game and a man whose courage had helped him crawl 200 yards to safety after being badly shot In the stomach during the Korean War.

Right at the start, McMillan put it to Davis: 'Harold, I can't tackle a fish supper and I'm no good in the air. But I can pass the ball. You can't do that, but you can win it. You do that, and look for me. I'll always be available.'

'BETWEEN THE TWO OF US WE SHOULD BE ABLE TO MAKE ONE GOOD PLAYER.'

Ian remains to this day a friend of Harold, who now runs a hotel up in Gairloch.

'He never got the credit he deserved. He worked so hard for the team and everyone else. And he really could play a bit as well, in his own solid way.'

Davis was also a handy man to have around when things got tough. Particularly in the European hot-spots.

'I can remember the game against Borussia in Germany where a guy called Bidurftig was giving me a really hard time. Next thing we knew, he was lying flat and was stretchered off with a jaw injury. Nobody saw what happened. But at the end of the game big Harold still had one of the guy's teeth imbedded in his hand.'

Ian also had a close-up of action man Davis at work in the infamous 'Battle of Seville', the European Cup first-round tie that ended in a right barney which involved all twenty-two players.

'There would have been more,' says Ian, who was sitting on the subs' bench watching. 'For the Seville subs all rose to get out of their seats in the low dug-out, but Harold put a stop to that by launching himself right at the lot of them. They never came out that trench again!'

Ian's career at Ibrox lasted just six years, but what years.

He was there when Rangers took the Championship in '58-59, '60-61, '62-63 and '63-64.

He played in the League Cup Final wins over Killie (2-0) in 1960 and Hearts (3-1 after a 1-1 draw) in 1961.

Player of the Year McMillan is congratulated by Rex of the *Sunday Mail.*
Late Rangers chairman John Lawrence looks on.

And there were three Scottish Cup triumphs. The 2-0 win
over Kilmarnock in '59-60; victory by the same score over St.
Mirren in '61-62 and the replay success over Celtic in 1962-63
when, after a 1-1 draw, which Ian missed, he was recalled for
the return match and played brilliantly as his team swept to a
3-0 win.

That was the Final which was dubbed the 'Saga of the Missing Ball.'

Ian tells the story: 'At the end of the game Jim Baxter picked
up the ball, stuck it up his jersey and refused to hand it over to
the referee.'

'Instead he gave it to me in the dressing room. Jim, despite
all his flamboyance, was a generous bloke and he felt that
since I was getting near the end of my career I should have the
ball.'

'The S.F.A. thought otherwise. I want my ball back, was more or less what secretary Willie Allan said. So to save any more fuss, I took it to Ibrox the next day and it was returned to Park Gardens.'

But now Ian can let everyone into a secret: he DOES have the ball.

'It was given to me by the S.F.A. when my playing days were over,' says Ian. 'So they weren't so heartless after all. It is one of my most treasured mementoes.'

Ian's six star-studded years came to an end on April 29, 1964 when he played against St. Johnstone in a League game at Perth. It wasn't a happy farewell — Rangers went down 1-0.

But the result didn't really matter — Rangers had already won the title. And the League Cup. Then came the Scottish Cup, to complete a fantastic triple-crown year.

McMillan shared a little in the success: he played in ten League games and three of the Scottish Cup ties, including the 1-0 semi-final victory over Dunfermline.

But he didn't feature in the Final, which Rangers won 3-1 in dramatic style. With only two minutes to go the score was 1-1 against Dundee, who had been inspired by goalkeeper Bert Slater. Then stunningly Ralph Brand and Jimmy Millar netted in the remaining two minutes just as a replay seemed certain.

Ian went back to his home-town team on December 2, 1964 for a fee of around £4,000. He served them again as player, until injury forced him out, coach, manager and now director.

'The longest walk in football' is how Ian describes the manager's stroll round the track at Broomfield from dressing room to dug-out.

'I gave the job up because I found I was taking the results as badly as the fans. I guess I just didn't have it in me to handle the criticism. I felt as upset as they did when things went wrong.'

He still watches Airdrie, plays a lot of golf when time allows and is the proud grandfather of three lively boys.

'It's too early yet to say if any will make a player,' he jokes.

He also runs his own painting company in Airdrie. But still finds time to look back in wonder at the golden age of Rangers in the McMillan-Baxter era.

'I played with a great team. We had so much success, so much enjoyment.'

'It's hard to pick out the best of the games, but I would say the night we demolished German side Borussia 8-0. It was an awful night, and the pitch was a mud-heap.'

'But I loved that. The slippier the better. I could use my shimmy and big defenders couldn't get a grip on the turf to stop. On a firm ground, they might get back to me for a second bite.'

'And our semi-final against Eintracht when we lost 6-3 at Ibrox was memorable. What a game. All right the Rangers fans didn't get the result they wanted, but they got nine goals and saw some brilliant goals.'

'As for great players .... well Jim Baxter was unique. He could be having a mediocre game, then suddenly turn up something brilliant which swung everything Rangers' way.'

Typically Ian doesn't have a lot to say about his own career.

He even dismisses a Rangers landmark — the club's 5,000th League goal — with a laugh. The honour fell to Ian on October 14, 1961.

His goal was the first in a 6-0 home win over Raith Rovers. Ian describes it this way: 'I went for a cross from the left, the ball hit somewhere round the bridge of my nose and took a funny bounce. I think the keeper might still have got it but for the fact that Ralph Brand ran across it and dummied beautifully. The credit belongs to him.'

Since Brand scored four goals that day, he got enough credits as it was.

So the last word on the modest McMillan comes from one of Rangers' all-time legends, Bob McPhail, who played with the greats in the 1920s and '30s and stayed on to watch Rangers over the next half-century.

'I never saw a better inside forward at Ibrox than Ian McMillan,' he declares.

Enough said.

INTERNATIONAL RECORD

FULL CAPS

1952
(with Airdrie)

Apr.	England	(Hampden)	1-2
Apr.	U.S.A.	(Hampden)	6-0
May	Denmark	(Copenhagen)	2-1

1955
(with Airdrie)

| Apr. | England | (Wembley) | 2-7 |

1961
(with Rangers)

| May | Czechoslovakia | (Bratislava) | 0-4 |

CHAPTER SIX

Jim Baxter

Jim Baxter reckons that if he were playing his football today in the glare of publicity which some newspapers direct towards the exploits of soccer stars, then he would have a reporter on permanent detachment.

Being Baxter, he would naturally offer the guy a bed.

'A double, of course', says the mischievous former Rangers and Scotland midfield genius. 'And probably something to keep it warm for him.'

Jim Baxter has always lived life in the fast lane.

Foot jammed on the pedal, window open to whistle at the passing girls with stops only for the boozer or betting shop.

'I had a helluva time. It was great while it lasted,' says Jim.

It is still lasting. He might not have the fortune any more to go with the fame, but Baxter's lifestyle in the south side of Glasgow is still the same.

The start of it all . . . Baxter joins his junior club, Crossgates Primrose.

'I never wanted to be a millionaire. Just live like one,' he says.

'I do what I like, when I like. I still wake up in the morning and say 'Great: what am I going to do today'.'

James Curran Baxter was always a single-minded character . . . even in his school days in Hill o' Beath in Fife.

But it was an event years later that was to shape Baxter's approach to life.

'I was only in my early 20s when John White was killed by lightning on the golf course,' says Jim.

'I can remember being at the funeral and seeing guys like Dave Mackay and Bobby Shearer, men as hard as you could get, being reduced to tears.'

'I never knew anyone who disliked John White. He was the model professional, lived just right. And he was killed because of change in his pocket or the metal zip on his trousers, for God's sake.'

'That made my mind up for me. I was going to enjoy everything that was going. I was going to have a right good kick at the ball.'

He has been playing keepy-up with life ever since.

And Baxter, being Baxter, never tried to hide his lifestyle.

He couldn't hide either the gift of being one of the most naturally talented footballers this country has ever produced.

His skill has unfortunately at times been overwhelmed by his shenanigans.

But those privileged to watch Baxter weave his magic in club, European and international football will never forget the sight.

How he managed it, is hard to say. He wasn't fast; couldn't tackle, didn't like chasing back to cover; hated training and looked sloppy as he drifted about the pitch with stockings slipping and jersey hanging loose over his shorts.

But give Baxter the ball and he not only could make it talk — it would recite the Gettysburg address.

It was a natural talent, one he could never pass on through coaching to anyone, which is why he shunned any offers of management or coaching which came to him at the end of his career.

Oh how times have changed. The signing of J. Baxter, £2-10-0!

'Give them a ball, and let them get on with it' is Baxter's advice to all and sundry.

His approach to football was simple. If he didn't have the ball, he could do nothing. Give him it, and then watch what happened.

He had developed this philosophy by the time he was 14 and playing for Beath High. But when the time came to leave school, there was no football career on the horizon . . . just a start as an apprentice cabinet maker.

That didn't last long. His pals who had gone down the pit were earning four times his wages, and even then Baxter knew the value of an extra pound in the pocket. Particularly when heading for a night out (albeit illegally) in the local hostelries.

Slim Jim, and he really was just that in those days, was playing only Sunday afternoon games until some pals started a boys' club.

They quickly won everything in sight — which in turn won Jim a place with the quaintly named Crossgates Primrose, the local junior team.

The records show that they paid Baxter 50 shillings to sign on. In reallly, it was £50 in used notes. An under-the-counter payment that Baxter promptly converted into a washing machine for his mother Agnes.

By 1957 Raith Rovers were on the scene, taking Baxter out on trial . . . against Rangers Reserves who sported such names as Ralph Brand, Jimmy Millar, Davie Wilson and the fearsome charging South African, Don Kichenbrand.

Big guns. But Baxter obviously did well enough to warrant being signed on part-time terms for the Kirkcaldy side, bringing him a princely £3 a week.

It didn't take long for Baxter to opt for full-time football, giving up his £7 a week down the pits. And it wasn't long either before his talent brought him a lot of attention.

'I was lucky in those early days at Raith to be surrounded by a squad of seasoned pros who protected me, helped me and let me get settled into senior football', says Jim.

An Under-21 cap against Wales in December 1958 was the first indication of the glory days that were to lie ahead.

That team — which lost 1-0 to Wales at Tynecastle — included names like Doug Baillie, Bert Slater, Duncan MacKay, Alex Young, Davie Sneddon, Davie Wilson.

It was also a game which gave him a taste for better things.

'I'd spent £15 getting myself a new suit and coat from Burtons, and thought I was a dandy. But somehow I was made to feel like a hick from the sticks. If you weren't with one of the big clubs then even a new suit wouldn't make you anything but a nobody.'

'I knew I was going for the big time after that.'

But there were a couple more years of learning to be done.

Manager of Raith Rovers was Bert Herdman, a legendary local figure who Baxter says should have been made 'Chancellor of the Exchequer' for his financial dealings on behalf of the club.

Captain Jim . . . a happy Baxter leads out Rangers at Ibrox.

'Bert had a stammer, and I can recall in my last season with Raith before I joined Rangers, that we actually beat them 3-2 at Ibrox before a 30,000 crowd.'

'After a game in Glasgow we always went to the Ivy Restaurant in Buchanan Street for high tea. You know — fish and chips or a sausage, bacon and egg.'

'When we got there, I asked Bert Herdman if the team

wasn't due a special bonus for beating Rangers at Ibrox. It hadn't happened too often before.'

'Bert said he would have to ask the directors. Went away and came back beaming to say: 'Right lads, I've done a deal for you. Forget the high tea, you can go à la carte'.'

Baxter didn't even know what à la carte meant. But within a few months he did. For he signed for Rangers. And from then on it was first class all the way . . . 'and just send the bill to Ibrox.'

The records show he signed for Rangers on June 21, 1960. In reality, Baxter had actually signed for £17,500 a few months earlier but the deal was not revealed.

'Something to do with a new tax year, I think,' says Jim.

Baxter had arrived. And so did a half-decade that was to be laden with honours and success for Rangers.

In his five years at Ibrox from 1960 to 1965, Baxter won TEN of the fifteen medals that were available in those years.

He has three championship medals ('61, '63, '64). Three Scottish Cup badges ('62, '63, '64). And four League Cup medals ('60, '61, '63, '64).

Baxter made his competitive debut against Partick Thistle at Ibrox in a League Cup section tie. Rangers won 3-1, and the golden days began. The teams that day were:

Rangers: Niven; Caldow, Little; Davis, Paterson, Stevenson; Scott, McMillan, Millar, Baxter, Wilson.

Partick Thistle: Freebairn; Hogan, Baird; Wright, Harvey, Donlevy; Smith, McParland, Wardlaw, Fleming, Ewing.

Within three months Baxter had won his first medal — Rangers beating Kilmarnock 2-0 at Hampden in the League Cup Final on October 29, 1960 with goals from Ralph Brand and Alex Scott.

Baxter's wages had gone up from £17 a week with Raith, to £22 with Rangers. But there was a lot more money than that to be made for a winning Ibrox team in bonuses.

However, within a couple of years the rebel bit in Baxter emerged, probably developed during the two years of National Service where he did very little serious army work but had his taste for the good life extended by touring with the Army side.

Private Baxter of the Black Watch — and sundry comrades

like Pat O'Connor of Kilmarnock and Davie Gibson of Hibs — were treated to nothing but the best, especially on overseas tours.

'Just at the end of my army time we had a memorable seven-week tour of the Far East. Hong Kong, Singapore, Saigon, Kuala Lumpur. It was a long way from Hill o'Beath, I can tell you.'

'I even managed to meet Rita Hayworth on that trip. Didn't get much chance to talk to her, mind you, she had a very jealous friend who looked capable of handling our whole army team on his own.'

Being stationed at Stirling (by some happy accident!) meant the Baxter brand of football was on display at Ibrox for most of his conscription period.

When his first season ended, Baxter also had added a League championship medal to his collection, the title taken by a point from Kilmarnock who had beaten Rangers home and away that season.

He also had time to sample the delights or otherwise (depending on the result) of Old Firm encounters.

His first taste was the dregs of defeat — Celtic coming to Ibrox on August 20, 1960 for a League Cup tie and inflicting a 3-2 defeat on Baxter and Co. just four days after Third Lanark had won 2-1 in a section tie at Cathkin.

Incredibly, that was the last time Baxter was on a losing side against Celtic in any of the three major competitions until five years later.

Rangers won the return leg of the League Cup meeting 2-1 at Parkhead on September 3. A week later they went back on League business . . . and blitzed Celtic 5-1.

'I can remember that there was nothing in it until more than a hour had gone,' says Baxter. 'We had scored through Alex Scott in the second minute but had been lucky to hold that lead as Steve Chalmers hit woodwork twice.'

'Then suddenly — click. We scored four goals inside twenty minutes and that was that.'

'We really had the 'hex' on Celtic during my time with Rangers.'

'I honestly never felt they were likely to beat us.'

'In fact, I used to kid on the Celtic players that I was getting letters of thanks from the supporters' wives for making sure their menfolk were home early on a Saturday since they were leaving the game before the end.'

Baxter was in fact friends, but not bosom pals, with many of the Celtic players, and could 'enjoy a pint with them.'

He also enjoyed a reasonable relationship with the Celtic fans.

'They never despised me the way they did some of the other Rangers players,' says Jim. 'They knew I basically couldn't care less about religion and also that I was using skill to beat Celtic. The kind of skill they liked to see in their own team.'

Between 1960 and 1965 Baxter played in ten League, five League Cup and three Scottish Cup games against the old rivals and was only twice on the losing side.

'We had a tremendously well balanced side,' says Jim. 'Ian McMillan and myself did the clever things in midfield. But we couldn't have done them without the support of strong, hard-working players like Bobby Shearer, Harold Davis and Jimmy Millar.'

'And smart operators like Eric Caldow, Ralph Brand, Alex Scott, Willie Henderson and Davie Wilson.'

'A lot of people like to criticise Scot Symon. I loved the man. He was the greatest Rangers supporter of all time. The club was everything to him.'

'He might not have been over-tactical, but he was from the old school and simply let players get on with it. If they were good enough to play for Rangers, they didn't need to be told much.'

'He kept the game simple. And it is a simple game for good players. He would tell the defence just to win the ball, don't do anything fancy and just move it on to McMillan or myself. It certainly worked.'

There are also those who say that by letting Baxter away with indiscretions in conduct and dress on and off the field, plus a lenient attitude towards the player's ever-increasing lax-

Private Baxter of the Black Watch on parade.

ity in training, Symon actually hindered rather than helped the player.

'I can't remember the number of times when I was up the stairs to see the boss to answer for my sins, particularly when it came to training. I never liked it. And I particularly didn't like the kind of pointless slog without the ball which the likes of Davie Kinnear and others of his time persisted with.'

'Sure I took a few liberties with Scot Symon's softer approach to me. But I gave the man back everything on the playing field.'

'And for those who say he should have been tougher . . . well, maybe then I wouldn't have played so well for him. I certainly never wanted to let the boss down, I can tell you.'

But even early into his Ibrox career Baxter's rebel touch, especially regarding payment for star players, was beginning to show through.

'I could never understand a system whereby we could play

in front of a 90,000 crowd paying good money — yet not get a penny extra in bonus if we happened to lose. There was nothing tying in crowds with cash in those days, and I resented that and was never short in letting Rangers know.'

'I used to try to get Bobby Shearer to go upstairs and make out a case, but Bobby was such a blue nose he would have played for Rangers for nothing.'

'Scot Symon used to say to me not to worry about money, that playing for Rangers would open a lot of doors. But I had seen too many ex-players who were broke and neglected. You can't eat medals.'

Baxter had several signing revolts before he finally left the club in 1965.

But before then he had added to the legend with one brilliant game after another for his club. And then for his country.

He won the first of his thirty-four international caps against Northern Ireland at Hampden on November 9, 1960 when the Scots won 5-2.

The team is worth noting: Leslie; McKay, Caldow; Mackay, Plenderleith, Baxter; Herd, Law, Young, Brand, Wilson.

Law, Caldow, Young and Brand (2) were the Scots scorers.

Baxter missed Scotland's next international, which was a lucky escape. THAT was the 9-3 defeat by England at Wembley on April 15, 1961.

He was in the following month against the Republic of Ireland for a 4-1 win at Hampden. And in from then on unless injury got in the way.

That Eire game, incidentally, was the first one to feature a half-back line which many consider to be as good as any Scotland has every produced . . . Crerand, McNeill, Baxter.

'A myth was created round that half-back line,' says Jim. 'We only played together seven times, you know, and lost three of those games.'

Maybe so, but there was something about that explosive mixture of temperament which captured the imagination. Explosive is the word, mind you. For many fans will recall the great Scotland sponge punch-up.

Scotland were in Belgium for a World Cup play-off against

Czechoslovakia in November 1961, and the game went to extra time.

'It was during one of the intervals that the trainer came on with his sponge. Nerves must have been frayed, for when Pat Crerand grabbed the sponge I snarled at him, saying there are eleven of us here and snatched it from him. We had a right little set-to before we were calmed down.'

'Paddy and I were mates, too. Just shows how the tension can get to you. Usually I wasn't affected, but I must have been that time.'

'I've seen big Ian Ure so nervous in the Scotland dressing room he couldn't tie his laces. Him a big fellow over 6ft tall and strong as a horse.'

For Baxter, all the world was a stage. And all the Scots loved this particular strolling player.

Particularly when he helped tease and defeat the English at Wembley as he did in 1963 and 1967.

Baxter recalls both with relish. The '63 game was, of course, the unfortunate scene of Eric Caldow's leg break early in the match.

The 100,000 crowd were then treated to an amazing exhibition as the ten-man Scots (no subs in those days) kept cool and won the game 2-1.

Baxter put the handicapped Scots ahead with a cracking left-foot drive in the first half, and was in such tremendous form that when the Scots were awarded a penalty acting captain Dave Mackay had no hesitation.

'You're on a high, Jim. You take it,' he said as he lobbed the ball to Baxter.

'I wonder if he would have been so confident if he had known that I had never taken a penalty before in senior football,' confesses Baxter.

'What a place to start. Wembley in an England-Scotland game. But the way I was feeling, I could have headed the spot kick in and still scored.'

That feeling of control, total mastery of the ball and the game was to be with Baxter on hundreds of occasions.

Like his return to Wembley in 1967 when the Scots faced

World champions England . . . and ended their unbeaten nine-teen-game run with a 3-2 victory that could easily have been far greater.

Baxter tormented the English, linking up with Billy Bremner in midfield. Controlling the flow of play and even having the cheek to indulge in a spot of 'keepy-up' in his own penalty area.

'I just wanted to bring them down a peg,' says Jim.

That point in time was clearly Baxter's best. For it was less than two weeks later he turned in what he says was his 'greatest ever performance.'

But there was no Wembley, Hampden, Ibrox or glamorous European setting for this virtuoso recital. It was Firhill on a re-scheduled Wednesday night fixture on April 17, 1963.

'Everything I tried came off. It was an uncanny feeling.'

'I could make the ball turn and twist; send people the wrong way; lay on chance after chance. If I wanted to pass the ball thirty yards, it went thirty yards. Precisely.'

'I don't think I ever played as well, and I was nearly in tears afterwards. I knew it was a performance which deserved a big-ger stage than Firhill.'

Davie Wilson didn't mind. He scored all four goals in the 4-0 win.

That same mystical magic was with Baxter again in what he rates as the best of the twenty-four European ties he played with Rangers in the dazzle days.

The setting was the Prater Stadium in Vienna, one of the most famous grounds in the world. A fitting setting this time for some vintage Baxter.

The date was December 8, 1964. The performance was one of Rangers' best-ever in Europe as they beat Rapid Vienna 2-0.

But for Jim Baxter this moment of triumph turned to per-sonal tragedy.

'The game was over as far as I was concerned,' says Jim. 'We had waltzed the Viennese dizzy on a mud-heap pitch. I laid on the first goal for Jim Forrest, and Willie Johnston, in his first European game on the Continent, set up the other for Davie Wilson.'

Another success against Celtic — Baxter with the 1964 League Cup.

'There was only half a minute to go and to be quite truthful I was actually walking OFF the pitch, heading for the touchline to nip up the tunnel.'

'Then the ball came my way again, and I was so casual I was getting out of the way to let it go over the line when this fellow Skocik came flying in to make a tackle and whacked me on the leg.'

'He didn't know I wasn't interested in touching the ball. But as soon as he hit me, I knew it was a break.'

Little did anyone know that the tackle was to finish Baxter. Not with football, for he was back in three months.

But there can be no doubt that the long lay-off started Baxter's career on the slide. The magic became well, if not mediocre, certainly somewhere short of dazzling.

Baxter wasn't the type to put in the real hard work needed to overcome this kind of injury. He had a deep loathing of training at the best of times and also the injury had made him even more aware of how short a footballer's playing span could be.

'I wanted more money. It was as simple as that.'

'I was getting £45 a week, I wanted £80. Scot Symon nearly had a coronary. I pointed out to him that Johnny Haynes was getting £100 a week with Fulham, drawing much smaller crowds than Rangers, and that there was no way he was more than twice the player I was.'

Three months after his injury Baxter was back for Rangers. Two months after that he left them.

Sunderland came with a £72,000 offer which Rangers accepted. And an offer to Baxter he couldn't refuse.

'I picked up £11,000 in my hand. Now that was REAL money in those days.'

But if the gold lay south, the golden days were behind him in the north.

His sojourn with Sunderland and then Notts Forest was bearably sucessful with the first club — a total disaster with the second.

The injury, his lack of enthusiasm for training over the years and his lifestyle all took a toll. Plus of course he was expected to WORK hard in England, not just to make himself available to take the ball and supply the class moves.

And, also, he is the first to admit that he didn't have a Harry Davis or a Bobby Shearer looking after his welfare when the hard men down south came looking for him during a game.

He lasted eighteen months at Sunderland and was then surprisingly transferred to Nottingham Forest for £100,000 in December, 1967 . . . again picking up a large slice of the transfer and increasing his wages.

Two of the all-time greats — Jim Baxter and Denis Law.

'I tried hard at Sunderland in the beginning, but it just never worked because the team wasn't suited to me and the players were not as good as the men I was with at Ibrox,' says Jim.

'Forest had finished second top of the table the previous season, so I thought they were the right club to join. I was wrong.'

Baxter's eighteen months at Nottingham brought no success, and a succession of stories about his off-field scrapes in clubs and pubs, particularly when accompanied by a new-found friend . . . West Indian cricketer Gary Sobers.

'I certainly enjoyed myself, but I didn't do much for Nottingham Forest,' recalls Jim.

But even he wasn't expecting to be given a free transfer eighteen months after his signing. And if that was a surprise, his return to Rangers under Davie White in May 1969 was even more so.

But once again, there was no way the clock could be put into reverse.

In addition, Rangers were a team struggling to get clear of the giant shadow being cast by Jock Stein's Celtic. A reversal of roles from Baxter's sunshine days.

Despite helping the team to a 2-1 win over the old rivals in the first game in their League Cup section, Baxter didn't play for the Ibrox men as they first of all lost at Parkhead in the return then dropped a point at home in a 3-3 draw with Raith Rovers to finish runners-up to the Parkhead side in the section.

Celtic also beat them 1-0 at Ibrox in the September League meeting and by early November they had won only six of their eleven League matches, and the end came for Davie White when they were beaten 3-1, home and away, by the Polish side Gornik in the Cup Winners Cup. .

'It was a disappointment to me that even in the good years I had at Ibrox we never won a European trophy,' says Baxter.

'But it really was hard to adjust from playing against Partick Thistle or Clyde on the Saturday, then go out on Wednesday and try to play the same way against a top Italian team.'

'It took British teams a dozen years of European experi-

The irrepressible Baxter shows the confident style that was his trademark.

ence before they cracked it — then once Celtic showed the way, others followed.'

After White went — Waddell came. And Baxter was going.

Waddell had been a great admirer of the Baxter play in the great days. But he knew they were past and was not in the mood to 'carry' any passengers as he set about rebuilding the club's fortunes.

Waddell joined Rangers on December 3, 1969. Baxter played against Hearts in the 2-1 win on December 6 at Tyne-castle and the 3-2 away win against Aberdeen on December 13.

And there it ended. He never showed in the first team again, was given a free transfer on April 28, 1970 and promptly set himself up in business in a pub a mile along the road from Ibrox.

His second stint had lasted less than a year and saw him play 14 League games, 4 League Cup ties and 4 European matches. Rangers won 14 of the 22 games, drew 3 and lost 5.

'But I knew within a week or so of Willie Waddell arriving my days were numbered,' says Baxter. 'He simply stopped talking to me.'

For a long time Baxter's publican days were rich and rewarding. But he never did learn to control his desire to go wherever the party was.

Ultimately this led to the loss of his business and the collapse of his marriage.

'My own worst enemy. But I'll never change now,' says Jim with a philosophical shrug.

He's still very much his own man, and gave up a lucrative job with the Stakis organisation because he felt it was restricting.

He goes to Ibrox when he can. Thinks Graeme Souness is doing a tremendous job, but has a lot to learn about Scottish football.

And firmly believes that even the multi-million pound side that Souness has built would have been demolished by: Ritchie; Shearer, Caldow; Greig, McKinnon, Baxter; Henderson, McMillan, Millar, Brand, Wilson.

Back again — Baxter rejoins Rangers, watched by manager Davie White and his assistant Willie Thornton.

'I don't think just money can put together a team. The spirit and the blend have to be right. Scot Symon bought in players like myself, Shearer, Millar and McMillan.'

But the rest of the team came up through the ranks after being recruited as boys.

'It would be foolish of Rangers to just buy and not build. They must bring on their own boys. There is a tremendous revival of support for them, which will make more and more youngsters want to be at Ibrox.'

'Even if only one in ten makes it . . . that one could be the new Jim Baxter.'

INTERNATIONAL RECORD

1960

Nov.	N. Ireland	(h)	5-2

1961

May	Rep. Ireland	(h)	4-1
May	Rep. Ireland	(a)	3-0
May	Czechoslovakia	(a)	0-4
Sept.	Czechoslovakia	(h)	3-2
Oct.	N. Ireland	(a)	6-1
Nov.	Wales	(h)	2-0
Nov.	Czechoslovakia (Brussels)		2-4 a.e.t.

1962

Apr.	England	(h)	2-0
May	Uruguay	(h)	2-3
Oct.	Wales	(a)	3-2
Nov.	N. Ireland	(h)	5-1

1963

Apr.	England	(a)	2-1
May	Austria	(h)	4-1
Jun.	Norway	(a)	3-4
Jun.	Rep. Ireland	(a)	0-1
Jun.	Spain	(a)	6-2
Nov.	Norway	(h)	6-1
Nov.	Wales	(h)	2-1

1964

Apr.	England	(h)	1-0
May	W. Germany	(a)	2-2
Oct.	Wales	(a)	2-3
Oct.	Finland	(h)	3-1
Nov.	N. Ireland	(h)	3-2

1965

Oct.	N. Ireland	(a)	2-3
Nov.	Italy	(h)	1-0
Nov.	Wales	(h)	4-1

1966

Apr.	England	(h)	3-4
Jun.	Portugal	(h)	0-1
Jun.	Brazil	(h)	1-1
Oct.	Wales	(a)	1-1

1967

Apr.	England	(a)	3-2
May	Russia	(h)	2-0
Nov.	Wales	(h)	3-2

Baxter also won five Scottish League honours, one Under-23 cap and played for the Rest of the World in the 1963 F.A. Centenary International at Wembley against England.

CHAPTER SEVEN

John Greig

John Greig, as far as I'm concerned, is the greatest Rangers player I have ever seen.

He wasn't as imposing a figure as the giant George Young; he wasn't quite as ferocious as Bobby Shearer or as quick as Eric Caldow.

Jim Baxter was a classier player and Davie Cooper more skilful.

But Greig had a mixture of all their qualities . . . plus a few of his own.

Dedicated. Determined. Strong. Unselfish. Honest and a 100 per cent professional in every deed and thought.

And a tremendous sense of humour . . . which only deserted him for a short time in his quarter of a century career with Rangers. That was in the latter days of his troubled time as manager of the club when pressures from within and without took their toll.

I'm happy to say that it didn't take long for the garrulous Greig to regain the touch which made him an inspiration in training and the dressing room — and an entertainer on long European trips.

Give John a microphone, and he took over. He obviously thought he was a combination of Bob Hope and Bing Crosby. And naturally he gave the performance 100 per cent.

But let's just say that in this particular field effort was no replacement for real ability!

Seriously, though, radio and TV viewers have sampled a taste of the Greig humour . . . and those who have ever heard him on a quiz or sports show have been offered even greater helpings and thoroughly enjoyed it.

John Greig in typical determined mood.

Greig, to this day, insists it was he who gave me my big break in newspapers.

Back in the early 1960s when I was a young reporter with the now sadly defunct Glasgow *Evening Citizen* and Greig an even younger rising star at Ibrox, I arranged to meet him and do the first real interview he had ever given.

We met at the Mokka coffee bar in Queen Street so that Greig could hop across the road and catch his train back to Edinburgh.

And right from the start it was clear that this strapping teen-ager with chubby cheeks and a haircut like his mother's scrubbing brush was a youngster who knew exactly where he was going — to the top.

Greig was determined to be a star. And even by then he was a dedicated Rangers man.

'I was lucky. I had great tutors to help me develop my under-standing of football and what it means to be a Rangers player,' says John.

'Every day I travelled back and forward to Edinburgh in a railway carriage which had players like Jimmy Millar, Ralph Brand and Billy Stevenson in it.'

'They talked, I listened. And I learned. They were tremen-dous characters and great players. They instilled into me the approach, thoughts and habits which were to keep me going as a player for nearly twenty years.

'I owe them a lot.'

He also owes me for that lunch. And a few others. For John always insists generously that I pay!

Greig was a Hearts fan and playing for Edina Hearts in Edinburgh when Rangers came and whipped him west.

It is a move he has never regretted.

'But there were one or two things I had to learn about play-ing for Rangers,' he recalls.

'I was working as an apprentice plating engineer for a year before I became a full-timer. One time I was working with my journeyman in Tennents Brewery in Duke Street, Edinburgh, and we went to the canteen for lunch.'

'I had just signed for Rangers, and my tradesman told the

Greig on the golf course — taking a break with his manager Scot Symon.

brewery boys this. It was a Friday, and I sat down to a plate of haddock and chips.'

'Before I could lift my knife and fork, this guy came up, lifted my plate and planked down steak pie and potatoes in front of me.'

'Rangers players don't eat fish on a Friday,' he declared.

'I had to ask what this was all about, and discovered that fish on a Friday was deemed to be a Catholic habit!'

'I hate steak pie — but I had to eat it!'

That was the first of many lessons this big teenager from Edinburgh was to learn about life as a Rangers player — and the inescapable link with religious bigotry which is the curse of life in the West of Scotland.

Living in Edinburgh, which Greig did until he became Rangers manager in the late 1970s, thankfully tended to be less perilous in this respect.

Just over a year after signing for Rangers, Greig was launched into his first-team career.

'I was due to have played in a Glasgow Cup game the season before, but missed it because of injury,' says Greig.

So it was against Airdrie in the League Cup at Ibrox on September 2, 1961 that Greig stepped into the side at inside right in place of the injured Ian McMillan.

And it was a scoring debut, too . . . he netted in the 10th minute to set Rangers off on a 4-1 win.

The teams on that debut day were:

Rangers: Ritchie; Shearer, Caldow; Stevenson, Paterson, Baxter; Scott, Greig, Christie, Brand, Wilson.

Airdrie: Dempster; Shanks, Keenan; Rankin, Johnstone, McNeil; Newlands, Storrie, Tees, Caven, Duncan.

A crowd of 32,000 saw a new star born. Greig was to play in eleven League matches, a Scottish Cup tie against Aberdeen at Pittodrie and two League Cup matches; and at the tender age of 18 got his first taste of European football.

He and another teenager Willie Henderson formed the right wing in the European Cup quarter-final first-leg meeting with Standard Liège in Belgium, which Rangers lost 4-1.

His League debut was against Falkirk at Ibrox on November 18th, 1961 when Jimmy Millar scored a hat-trick as the Light Blues swept to a 4-0 win. The following week Greig scored the first of his seven League goals that season in a 3-2 win over Dundee United at Tannadice.

'That was a phenomenal team to learn the game with,' says Greig.

'We were playing 4-2-4 in those days before anyone had heard of it.'

'Baxter and McMillan were wonderful ball-players and read the game so well. Henderson or Scott on the right gave pace and drive; Davie Wilson had a nose for goals and Millar and Brand were a tremendous combination up front of strength, speed and finishing skill.'

Greig has nothing but respect for the then boss Scot Symon, whom he describes as 'the last of the lounge suit managers'.

Celtic have scored . . . and John Greig doesn't like it!

E

'Scot conducted himself in a manner which had to impress you. He was a gentleman, and he was instrumental in giving me principles by which I still operate to this day.'

'He made Rangers play a system which suited the players available. Too many teams nowadays have a system and try to make the wrong men work it.'

'Scot didn't join in the daily training routine. But when he did turn up at the side of the track a couple of times a week, you could see the effect it had on players. They doubled up on their efforts.'

It's now part of the Ibrox folklore that it was during a close-season tour of Russia, in 1962, that the boy Greig dug himself a trench in front-line football with Rangers.

'You need the breaks as well as ability in football. I got my break that year,' says Greig.

'Jim Baxter couldn't go because of National Service commitments. Billy Stevenson had walked out on the club and gone to Australia — so the chance was there there for me.'

And he took it. Despite his tender years and lack of experience, he was a powerful figure in the tour which saw Rangers beat Moscow Lokomotiv 3-1, Tiblisi 1-0 and finish with a 1-1 draw against Russian champions Kiev.

The thousands of Rangers fans who had followed the tour via the newspapers were enthralled — and some 10,000 of them turned up at Glasgow Airport to greet the Icelandair flight which brought Rangers home.

It was clear a space in the side was going to have to be made for Greig. And although he wasn't automatically in the first team at the start of 1962-3, he couldn't be kept out, and eventually it was big Harold Davis who had to give way in the right-half position.

Greig was on his way. He played twenty-seven League games, five League Cup, seven Scottish Cup and half a dozen others. He scored ten goals and at the age of 20 had won his first League championship medal and first Scottish Cup badge, as Rangers walloped Celtic 3-0 in the replay at Hampden.

Mine at last! Greig keeps a tight grip on the Cup Winners Cup.

Incidentally, a total of nearly A QUARTER OF A MILLION fans watched the two Old Firm games at Hampden that year.

The next year was vintage stuff — bringing Greig the FIRST of the three trebles he was to win over a fifteen-year period at Ibrox. He's Scotland's only triple treble man. It also brought him the first international recognition — a League Cap against the Irish League in Belfast, alongside team-mates Baxter, Henderson, Brand and Wilson.

The rise and rise of John Greig continued. In that season

Rangers beat Celtic twice in the League, twice in the League Cup and knocked them out of the Scottish Cup.

The star of success was shining brightly over Ibrox . . . and Greig.

He won Under-23 caps against Wales and England, both games lost away from home, and then on April 11, 1964 made his full Scotland debut.

'A winning one, too. And against England. That's always worth remembering,' says John. 'Big Alan Gilzean got the only goal — with a header of course.'

And for 21-year-old John Greig, it was the start of a run of twenty-one consecutive internationals for Scotland.

'I was lucky to be playing in a Scotland side packed with great players,' says Greig.

'Imagine what we could do nowadays with a team that had the likes of Pat Crerand, Jim Baxter, Billy McNeill, Willie Henderson, Denis Law, Alan Gilzean, Billy Bremner, Davie Wilson, Dave Mackay, Eddie McCreadie, Alex Hamilton and Charlie Cooke.'

'The list of fine players seemed endless.'

It must be pointed out that despite this roll of honour, Scotland still contrived to lose games they shouldn't have because of their own weaknesses, and still others because of call-offs by key players.

The 1965 World Cup qualifying campaign provides a couple of illustrations. Greig and the other Scots had two wins over Finland and an away draw against Poland behind them when they faced the Poles at Hampden in the return game.

Leading 1-0 for most of the game, the Scots contrived to lose two goals in the last ten minutes.

That left two very tough games to come against Italy, and it was on the night of November 9, 1965 that John Greig was forever given a place in the hearts of *all* Scottish fans, not just Rangers supporters.

Greig, with the true professionalism that was to mark his entire career, had agreed to a request from acting Scotland team boss Jock Stein to play at right back against the fancied Italians at Hampden.

A hero's salute: 70,000 crammed Ibrox for John's testimonial game.

'If you think I can do it — I'll do it,' said John.

He was told to mark danger man Barison. Which he did. He was told to look for a chance to have a pot at goal. Which he did ... coming steaming upfield two minutes from the end to meet a crossfield pass and crash a 25-yard rocket into the net for the winner.

'The scenes were chaotic. There were more than 100,000 fans going daft. The players were scarcely any better,' recalls John. Even Jock Stein was carried away — he landed up in the bath fully clothed!

But in typical Scotland style, the euphoria was dispelled sharply in the return game a month later.

It was to be John Greig's first game as captain of Scotland. But he was the leader of a strange-looking team. Injuries at the last minute ruled out Denis Law and Willie Henderson and Jim Baxter.

And when the two first-choice goalkeepers were also ruled out Jock Stein had to go to Burnley to bring in Adam Blacklaw for his third and last cap, and also to resort to a formation which had big Liverpool centre half Ron Yeats wearing the No. 9 jersey but operating in defence.

The inevitable result against the talented Italians was a 3-0 drubbing and a World Cup exit.

But for John Greig the disappointment was tempered by his elevation to the captaincy . . . a job he was to fill with typical Greig leadership and enthusiasm.

'There were bad times, but there were a lot of magic moments, too,' says John who was to lead Scotland on eleven occasions before losing the job to Billy Bremner . . . then regaining it again two years later for another two games. And, in a final tribute to his qualities, he was recalled for one game against Denmark in 1976 and bowed out as captain with a 3-1 win.

The goal against Italy is the public's favourite memory. For John it was leading Scotland to a 3-2 win over England at Wembley in April 1967.

'There's always something extra about winning at Wembley. But England were World Champions. They hadn't lost in nineteen games and we were given no hope.'

'It was Bobby Brown's first game in charge. And we destroyed England. It should have been more than 3-2. Jim Baxter was magnificent, of course. He even taunted England by playing keepy-uppie at the edge of our own penalty area. I must say I wasn't too impressed at the time!'

'But that was Jim — arrogant to the end. The scenes were chaotic when it ended, with the fans on the pitch taking home lumps as souvenirs. And the goalposts went, too.'

'But all I could think about was my brother and his wife in the stand, how, as a boy, I used to watch him going off to Wembley wearing his tammy. And here was I captain of the team that had just defeated the World Champions.'

'It's something I'll never forget.'

Incidentally, one of the invaders doing a spot of gardening at Wembley that year was a big lad from Stonehouse called Tom Forsyth . . . later to move from Motherwell to join Greig at Ibrox and play against England as well.

Medal man: A proud John Greig accompanied by wife
Janette and son Murray, shows off his MBE.

In the mid-60s, a change was coming over Scottish football. The great Rangers treble team was breaking up, with Baxter, McMillan, Brand, Millar, Shearer and Caldow all departing.

And Celtic were now under the guiding influence of the man who was to become the greatest manager of all . . . Jock Stein.

It was in the Stein-dominated years that the real strength of John Greig's character was tested. And he emerged with head held high.

For virtually five years he, along with able companion Ronnie McKinnon at centre-half, had to battle on week in week out with little to show for their efforts except sweat.

The Scottish Cup victory over Celtic in 1966, in a replay, was the only reward for the honest toil — a cracking shot from Danish full back Kai Johansen winning the trophy for the 19th time.

Greig was also honoured as Player of the Year by the Scottish Football Writers . . . an award he was to receive again a decade later in more rewarding times.

During those five years in the trophy wilderness, it would have been easy for Greig to give up. But he never thought of quitting Rangers.

'They were my team, my life. I knew the pendulum would swing back our way. But I didn't really think it would take five years.'

The axe swung, too, at Ibrox. Scot Symon went: sacked when the team were top of the table, but while Celtic were playing for the World Club championship. There had been talk of easing his burden as manager, and Eddie Turnbull turned down the chance of moving in as his assistant.

Coach Bobby Seith went with Symon, and assistant manager Davie White, recruited from Clyde a few months earlier, was given a step up. Two years later he went as well, without having won a trophy in that time.

Players were coming and going as well. Greig stayed on firm.

'Mind you, I did learn a long time later from Howard Kendall that at one point Everton wanted to buy me — but Scot Symon told them I wasn't for sale. That's when Everton then went and bought Kendall from Preston.'

Greig has no doubt that he wouldn't have moved anyway.

'I was enjoying living in Edinburgh. I was making good money and a lot of perks. I don't think I needed anything more.'

Just a chance to break free from the ever-growing shadow of Celtic, who beat Rangers into second place in the League championship five times in a row from 1966. And defeated them in two Scottish and two League Cup finals.

The first chink of light came in October 1970 when 16-year-old Derek Johnstone headed in the only goal of the game to beat Celtic and give Rangers the League Cup.

Greig's the Boss — and no one's going to forget it!

By this time Rangers were under new management — the formidable team of Waddell and Wallace. The former set about dragging the club set-up into modern times; the latter set about restoring fitness, commitment and pride.

But it was to be a long, hard slog with many disappointments along the way on the domestic front.

Celtic were still unconquerable in the League. And
although the Parkhead fans were enjoying every minute of it
all, and loved nothing better than to 'roast' Greig, whose total
commitment at times left a scattering of bruised players
behind him as he played as hard, but as fairly, as he knew.

But the Celtic fans also knew a great club man when they
saw one: and demonstrated this in remarkable fashion on September 16, 1972 in a League match being played at Hampden
because of ground work at Parkhead.

Greig remembers it well.

'Celtic had given us another hammering, and were leading
3-0 by just after the break. But I refused to give in, and in the last
minute got through their defence to score a goal.'

'The cheers from the Celtic end started out as ironic — but
then they realised I was doing for my club what they would
expect their players to do for theirs. And they really did give me
a reception.'

Not quite like the reception he received from the same
Parkhead punters at one New Year match when he was
switched to left back on a very hard, slippery surface and came
into close contact on many occasions with wee Jimmy
Johnstone.

Including one famous tackle where Johnstone vanished
off the pitch and into a pile of hay that had been taken off the
match surface a few hours earlier.

Greig likes to describe that as 'the last straw' for the Parkhead fans.

'They fairly let me know what they thought. And the letters
that came in were something else. But, truthfully, I hardly
touched Jinky. He was so light and bouncy that the slightest
tackle would send him flying.'

That's Greig's story, and he's sticking to it.

But it's no coincidence that when you ask him to name the
best player he played with his immediate reply is: 'Jimmy Johnstone. I could keep him up in the air for minutes on end!'

Before Rangers finally broke the Celtic grip in 1974-75, they achieved the long-sought European success.

Having failed twice before, Greig was determined that the Rangers fans would get the trophy they wanted when the team reached the Final of the Cup Winners Cup in Barcelona in May, 1972.

He and his mates succeeded. But the well-recorded events as thousands of Rangers fans clashed in ugly scenes with Spanish police turned the dream into a nightmare.

Greig's vision of parading the Cup before the fans was replaced with a shameful handing over of the trophy, and the other players' medals, in a dingy room under the stand.

'It was the biggest anti-climax of my life. I was in tears. All the hard work in getting there, beating Rennes from France; Sporting Lisch from Portugal; Torino from Italy and Bayern Munich from Germany . . . all that effort and fine play was forgotten. As was our showing against Dynamo Moscow in the Final.'

'All lost in a needless scene that could have been avoided by commonsense on both sides.'

To add injury to insult — Greig had the additional pain of being injured by one of his own fans.

'I had played on for quite a few weeks with a broken bone in my foot, and hadn't fully recovered. Then during the stampede at the end, a supporter stood on my foot and broke another bone.'

'I didn't discover this till a week later or so when I was on holiday in Jersey with Alfie Conn, Alex Miller and Bud Johnston. They wanted to have a kick about on the beach — I tried, and discovered suddenly I couldn't walk.'

Greig's offhand dismissal about playing with a broken bone in his foot reflects just one of the many times he soldiered on carrying an injury.

There was another example during the same season. And John still bears the scars to remind him.

'We were preparing down at Largs for the second leg of the game against Rennes, when I turned and ran after a ball which had passed me.'

'I didn't see a bench right behind me. But I certainly felt it. I landed chin first on it, and of course the rest of the lads doubled up with laughter. But when I didn't move they came over to see what was going on.'

'And when they rolled me over, Colin Stein said it was as though I had two mouths — and both were bleeding.'

Greig had split his chin so badly he needed nine stitches. The bench didn't fare too well, either. It was broken!

'The local doc came in, stitched me up and sent me to bed with some painkillers. I played that night, but I'm not sure if I knew what was going on.'

'Because of the injury, I couldn't shave. So I made up the story of not taking the beard off until we won the Cup. But even today I can still nick the scar tissue when I'm shaving.'

Greig's patient wait for the return of the good times at Ibrox was rewarded in 1974-75 when the team won the championship for the first time in eleven years. That win was the springboard which Jock Wallace used to catapult his team to the treble in 1975-76.

The glory days were back. And Greig basked in it all.

He was even more delighted when the team did the triple crown feat again in 1977-78, in what turned out to be his last year as a Rangers player.

Greig had no idea as he held the Scottish Cup aloft on Saturday, May 6, 1978 that eighteen days later he would be finished as a player. And started as a manager.

Jock Wallace's decision to quit because he felt he was not being rewarded for the success he had brought Rangers came on May 23. Next day Greig was manager.

In eighteen years as a player he played 857 senior games for Rangers; won four League championship medals, five Scottish Cup medals and four League Cup badges. Plus of course that European medal and 44 Scotland caps.

And, most importantly of all to him, he was awarded the M.B.E. at Buckingham Palace in 1977: 'the proudest day of my life,' he says.

It's a glorious record. One that it was fully expected he would enhance as a manager. But it didn't happen.

The glittering prizes: Greig toasts a five-trophy triumph at the end of his first season as manager.

Oh, it all began well. The League Cup was taken in March with a 2-1 win over Aberdeen. The Scottish Cup followed with victory over Hibs.

But then the team also went to Parkhead in the last League game of the season a point behind leaders Celtic and looking for victory to complete a first season treble.

Instead they tumbled to a 4-2 defeat, with Celtic reduced to ten men after John Doyle was ordered off.

Maybe that gives a clue to the unhappy times that followed. The Rangers players 'bottled' the chance. Would they have if Greig had been on the field?

His biggest problem turned out to be finding someone to replace himself as an inspirational figure.

'I tried Derek Johnstone as captain, because he really had been earmarked for the role,' says Greig. 'On reflection it was a mistake. I should have given the job to Sandy Jardine.'

Greig also set about altering the playing style. He wanted more emphasis on skilful build-up play, and his first step towards this was to put a halt to the sight of big Peter McCloy shelling the opposition goalmouth with his howitzer kick-outs.

'Even in training I insisted the keepers throw the ball out and play started from the back,' says John. 'I loved the way the Dutch played. I wanted to have a team that not just won, but entertained as well.'

But times were changing. So were the players' attitudes with freedom of contract. The club loyalty which Greig felt — and he believes he must have inherited this from his father who worked for forty-five years with Bairds the Bootmakers in Edinburgh — wasn't present in many of the newer generation of Rangers men.

The dressing-room harmony that Greig fostered as a player was no longer present, and some of his former team-mates 'went sour' as he puts it.

Greig tried all he knew to improve the situation. He worked non-stop. Signed new players, cleared away some of the older ones.

But victories in the '81 Scottish Cup against Dundee United with a blistering performance in a 4-1 replay victory and a 2-1 League Cup success over the same team the following year were not enough for the new generation of fans coming along to Ibrox.

They too readily forgot Greig's great years. The pain and the sacrifice. The only sacrifice they wanted now was Greig himself.

He always maintained the strain was not telling on him. But you could see it in his face, the greying of his hair and the loss of much of that breezy spirit.

Several times he wanted to go, but was persuaded to stay on. Eventually on October 28 Greig finally gave way and resigned.

'I never regretted taking the job. It came sooner than I planned. I wanted to go to America or somewhere and coach for a while.'

'But when you're offered the biggest club job in the land, you can't say no.'

'Eventually however it became clear to me that my family was suffering. My son was getting a hard time, even at a private school in Glasgow.'

'The club was suffering too. I knew it was time for a change for Rangers' good. But I wanted to leave with pride and dignity.'

Which he did. Leaving behind a chairman in Rae Simpson who had tears in his eyes when he read out the announcement to the journalists who had gathered at Ibrox.

'A sad day for Rangers' is how he described it. A sad day for Greig too.

But after taking a week or so to gather his thoughts, he turned to finding a new career. And he has, as travel agent, raconteur, radio and TV broadcaster and charity fund raiser.

'I don't miss the game at all now,' says Greig.

'Football owes me nothing. It gave me everything I have, and I tried to put as much back. The game and I are quits.'

'I would advise any young man who has the ability to have a go. But dedicate himself. The only way I played for eighteen seasons was hard work and watching my diet as I got older.'

'But that doesn't mean to say I didn't enjoy myself.'

'I know that I can go anywhere in the world and meet friends. I'll never just be John Greig. I'll always be John Greig of Rangers — and that's the way I like it.'

He could have stayed on in football management. But didn't have the wish or the will for that.

'I must have had ten offers to become a manager after I left Rangers. Some from abroad. But I just wouldn't consider them.'

'In fact, I was approached FOUR YEARS after I had given up.'

'But I knew when I quit Rangers I would never be a manager again. I would have been cheating any other club sitting out there on the bench.'

'My heart just would not have been in it.'

Greig has a host of memories: LIKE the 70,000 people who turned out at Ibrox for his testimonal game in 1978. 'The last capacity crowd at the old Ibrox before the new stadium was built,' recalls John. The £75,000 he received set him up for life, and has given him an abiding interest in stocks and shares.

LIKE the magic moment when he and Derek Johnstone set big Tom Forsyth up nicely on a flight across the Atlantic. Forsyth had been called a cabhorse by Manchester United's Tommy Docherty, and on the flight to America first Greig and then Johnstone posing as reporters had Forsyth on the intercom asking him his views.

'Big Tam was amazed at how they had managed to find the number. And he was worried about what it was costing the reporters. When he discovered it was a send-up I had to make sure never to be caught in a lift with him for the next four weeks.'

LIKE the moment in a game during a trip to Australia where an Aussie player deliberately tried to maim Greig. Who promptly pursued the guy upfield, with the ball passing over the two of them.

'When I caught up with him I was red-faced with anger. 'Your marks card,' I said warningly. Unfortunately Derek Johnstone was standing there and burst out laughing. 'What the hell does your marks card mean?' he said. I had to give up and laugh myself at that point.'

Greig is now a regular traveller with Rangers — and other Scottish clubs — on their European trips. But he has never yet got the hang of fancy foods.

He can be seen munching chocolate bars and eating dry corn flakes — he doesn't trust the milk — in all corners of the continent.

But he can fairly tackle a cheeseburger, as I witnessed once again when I last bought him lunch.

Mind you, I owe him another. After the meal he dragged me into a local bookies to back a horse owned by a pal of his. I won £30.

That'll buy a lot of cheeseburgers — which is surely not too much to offer the greatest of the Rangers greats.

INTERNATIONAL RECORD

1964

Apr.	England	(h)	1-0
May	W. Germany	(a)	2-2
Oct.	Wales	(a)	2-3
Oct.	Finland	(h)	3-1
Nov.	N. Ireland	(h)	3-2

1965

Apr.	England	(a)	2-2
May	Spain	(h)	0-0
May	Poland	(a)	1-1
May	Finland	(a)	2-1
Oct.	N. Ireland	(a)	2-3
Oct.	Poland	(h)	1-2
Nov.	Italy	(h)	1-0
Nov.	Wales	(h)	4-1
Dec.	Italy	(a)	0-3

1966

Apr.	England	(h)	3-4
May	Holland	(h)	0-3
Jun.	Portugal	(h)	0-1
Jun.	Brazil	(h)	1-1
Oct.	Wales	(a)	1-1
Nov.	N. Ireland	(h)	2-1

1967

Apr.	England	(a)	3-2
Oct.	N. Ireland	(a)	0-1
Nov.	Wales	(h)	3-2

1968

Feb.	England	(h)	1-1
May	Holland	(a)	0-0
Oct.	Denmark	(a)	1-0
Nov.	Austria	(h)	2-1
Dec.	Cyprus	(a)	5-0

1969

Apr.	W. Germany	(h)	1·1
May	Wales	(a)	5·3
May	N. Ireland	(h)	1·1
May	England	(a)	1 1
May	Cyprus	(h)	8·0
Sept.	Eire	(a)	1·1
Oct.	W. Germany	(a)	2·3
Nov.	Austria	(a)	0·2

1970

Apr.	Wales	(h)	0·0
Apr.	England	(h)	0·0
Nov.	Denmark	(h)	1·0

1971

Feb.	Belgium	(a)	0·3
May	Wales	(a)	0·0 sub.
May	N. Ireland	(h)	0·1
May	England	(a)	1·3

1975

Oct.	Denmark	(h)	3·1

CHAPTER EIGHT

Derek Johnstone

Derek Johnstone leaped straight into the history books at the age of 16 years and 355 days.

That's how old he was when he rose to meet a Willie Johnston cross at Hampden on October 24, 1970 . . . beating Celtic captain Billy McNeill and the highly experienced Jim Craig to the ball. And sending it flying past goalkeeper Evan Williams.

That goal gave Rangers the League Cup, their first trophy for five years. And it put the strapping Johnstone into the record books as the youngest player ever to score a winning goal in a national Final.

'I was a legend before my own lifetime,' jokes Derek.

Derek Johnstone —
he could never resist
clowning.

But he then confesses that in the main that Hampden game 'just passed me by'.

'I don't recall much of it at all. Probably I was in a state of shock about playing in the first place.'

'I only learned on the Friday afternoon 24 hours before the game that I was in the team.'

'Because I was still living in Dundee, my train for home was later in the afternoon and I usually spent the lunch hour in the boot room at Ibrox.'

'I was sitting there reading the paper when the boss Willie Waddell and coach Jock Wallace came in. They had obviously been upstairs making the decision to play me.'

'The gaffer told me I was in — stuck four complimentary tickets in my top pocket and told me to bring my mother and father.'

'He then gave me some impossible advice: go home and get a good night's sleep!'

There was never any danger, incidentally, of Derek's parents not being at the game. They knew he was in the first team pool, and were already Hampden-bound . . . in a 44-seater bus.

'They called it the DJ special,' says Derek. 'All my brothers and their pals had decided to be at the game, even though most of them were Dundee United fans. And there were enough friends and Rangers supporters in the neighbourhood to make sure the bus was full.'

It was a happy bus that made the trip back to Dundee.

'But I couldn't really answer all the questions about the game,' says Derek. 'Everything was a bit of a blur. I can remember watching the flight of Bud Johnston's cross. I knew there were a couple of Celtic men with me . . . and the next thing I knew I had connected and the ball was in the net. The only other thing I can recall is Johnston cheekily sitting on the ball near the end of the game.'

Derek wasn't given the opportunity of explaining his recollections to the waiting football writers after the game.

The Ibrox management team had decided to make sure this young high-flyer stayed firmly on the ground, and keep him away from too much publicity.

'I was hustled straight out of the door and past the reporters with Jock Wallace literally holding my arms behind my back,' says Derek.

'One writer asked me: 'What about the goal?'

'Jock Wallace answered for me: 'What about the ones he missed?'

The protective arm of Jock Wallace was to shelter Johnstone time and again over the years. He was also inclined, as Derek puts it, 'to shake you warmly by the throat at times'.

'But you always played for the man. He could get 100 per cent effort from everyone in those early days at Ibrox,' says Derek.

So at the age of 16, Johnstone was a medal winner.

'But I nearly didn't have it for long.' he recalls.

'Right after the Hampden game I went on a Youth trip to Iceland, and took my medal with me. I didn't want to have it stolen, so I hid it right at the back of a drawer in my hotel room.'

Naturally I forgot all about it — until I was on the plane home. Next day I was nearly in tears when I went to tell Willie Waddell. He just looked at me over his specs, and said to leave it with him. I got the medal back within three days.'

Contrary to popular belief, the Hampden Final was not Derek's first-team debut for Rangers. Nor did he score his first goal that day.

A month earlier the big teenager had been put into the first team in place of the injured Colin Stein for a League match against lowly Cowdenbeath at Ibrox.

'I think I had played about eight reserve games and was scoring goals, so the boss decided that it was worth taking a chance on me against Cowdenbeath,' says Derek.

'And my memories of this match are more vivid than the Hampden Final.'

'I scored twice, once in each half. And I can recall John Greig scoring twice as well — hitting one shot from twenty yards which nearly broke the bar and following up to get the rebound. I can also remember it was pouring that day.'

'For me it was unforgettable. There was a crowd of about 30,000 and I kept looking round at the men I was playing with, and finding it hard to believe it was really happening.'

The teams in that 5-0 win for Rangers were:

Rangers: McCloy; Jardine, Miller; Greig, McKinnon, Jackson; Henderson, Conn, Johnstone, MacDonald, Fyfe.

Cowdenbeath: Wylie; McLaughlan, Jack; Ferguson, Kinnell, Moore; Laing, Dickson, Mullen, Taylor, Ross.

It is also worth recording the League Cup Final teams from that Hampden clash in October:

Rangers: McCloy; Jardine, Miller; Conn, McKinnon, Jackson; Henderson, MacDonald, Johnstone, Stein, Johnston.

Celtic: Williams; Craig, Quinn; Murdoch, McNeill, Hay; Johnstone, Connelly, Wallace, Hood, Macari.

A crowd of 106,263 watched the game.

Johnstone's career was launched on a record-making start.

And records were to stay part of his style. By the time he finished playing for Rangers — after his second signing for the club — he had played 634 games for them, and scored a post-war record of 224 goals.

And 131 of them came in League competition, to make him the top scorer in this department in post-war games.

Which is impressive considering that he managed to out-shoot legendary players like Ralph Brand, Jimmy Millar, Billy Simpson, Max Murray, Jim Forrest . . . and Willie Thornton, although it should be pointed out that Thornton's post-war total of 109 doesn't take into account his pre-war performances, or the fact that from 1940-46 he was on active service.

Mind you, Johnstone himself might have had a lot more goals had he not suffered from a 'split personality'. He could never make up his mind whether to be a centre-forward or centre-half.

'Basically I preferred to play at the back, and come to meet the ball,' says Derek.

'But when you have a centre-forward who is scoring a lot of goals, and he wants to play centre-half it's a bit like comedians who want to do Hamlet on stage.'

'For quite a while I shifted back and forwards, and I think in the end my career suffered a bit from that. Certainly my international career did.'

The goal that became a legend. The 16-year-old Johnstone beats Celtic's Jim Craig and Billy McNeill to head the winner in the 1970 League Cup Final at Hampden.

'Probably this was my own fault. The year Scotland went to Argentina under Ally McLeod is a perfect example.'

'I had scored 41 goals that season, but I can remember in a Scotland get-together at Dunblane telling Ally that I really wanted to play centre-half.'

'Maybe if I'd kept quiet, I would have played in Argentina instead of just being a substitute. Mind you, on reflection maybe it wasn't a bad thing not to have played!'

Johnstone's versatility was such that he believes he is the only man ever to play for Scotland at both centre-half and centre-forward.

'I know John Charles did it often for Wales, but I don't think anyone else has done this for Scotland,' says Derek.

Indeed, the first five of his full Scotland honours were all at double centre-half in a formidably physical partnership with Manchester United's Jim Holton.

'The good, the bad and the ugly,' quips Derek. 'And big Jim was the latter two!'

They were paired together first in the Home International series in 1973, and got away to a good start with a 2-0 win over Wales. But the next four matches were all lost by the odd goal — N. Ireland (1-2) and then England, Switzerland and Brazil all by 0-1.

That was the end of his sojourn in defence. His next two Scotland appearances were as substitute in attack — against East Germany in 1974 and Sweden in 1975.

'They took off a couple of promising boys called Dalglish and Souness to let me play,' says Derek.

Humour is never far away when Johnstone is about.

He enjoys more daft puns than any player I've ever known, and startled the former Prime Minister James Callaghan at the 1978 Player of the Year dinner in Glasgow.

Johnstone was the Football Writers' choice that year, and was presented with the trophy by Mr Callaghan. Who then sat bewitched and amused while DJ made a hugely funny acceptance speech, which included producing a £1 from his pocket, and letting it drop on to the table in front of the distinguished Parliamentarian, at the same time informing him that this was an example of the 'floating pound'.

Nowadays listeners to his match summaries on Radio Clyde are subjected to some of his tortuous puns. They have not improved over the years, I can assure you!

But let me take you back near the beginning again.

Johnstone was just a 14-year-old schoolboy when Davie White signed him for Rangers in 1968. But already the signs of the prolific scorer had attracted a lot of attention, and this strapping boy was in fact training with Dundee United while playing for Linlathen High School and St. Francis Boys' Club.

'I was a United fan, as were my brothers. But I got bored with just running round the track a couple of nights a week. I could be playing up to four or five times a week with various competitions, and didn't enjoy just slogging round the pitch.'

It would be fair to say that never at any time did DJ enjoy the hard slog of training.

But his scoring ability was such that the Clink brothers — Bob and Danny — who ran St. Francis Boys' Club were forever having to seek out Derek and drive him to games to make sure he made it.

'I could be playing five or six times a week, and quite frequently was simply too knackered to bother with another match,' says Derek. 'But they would turn up for me, sometimes so late that I only went on for the second half!'

By the time he was called up to Ibrox in 1970, he had won schoolboy honours against England, Ireland and Wales. And he arrived at Rangers to discover the club under new management . . . Willie Waddell having succeeded Davie White, and with the formidable Jock Wallace as his assistant.

'Jock was really something else. He was first of all a bluenose. He used to regale us with these tales of his times in the jungle in Malaya when he would send one of his men up a palm tree with an aerial so that he could hear the Rangers score on the radio,' says Derek.

Johnstone was to become an essential part of the highly successful side being built up under the Waddell-Wallace partnership.

He played fourteen full and made seven substitute appearances in that 1970-71 season, scoring eight goals.

And within a year was playing his part in the only Rangers team yet to win a European trophy.

Yet he might never have played in that historic Cup Winners Cup triumph over Moscow Dynamo in Barcelona.

'Injury to other players got me in,' says Derek.

'I didn't play in any of the first four ties against Rennes and Sporting Lisbon. But then Ronnie McKinnon broke his leg in Portugal in the second leg, and by the quarter-final games against Torino I was in the team.'

Johnstone wore the No. 8 jersey against the Italians in Turin — but operated alongside Colin Jackson in defence. The result was a 1 - 1 draw, and Johnstone was still in the side when Rangers then swept past the Italians with an Alex MacDonald goal at Ibrox and faced the German cracks Bayern Munich in the semi-finals.

'I was given the job of marking Uli Hoeness in the first leg, and I must say so myself but I did a real good job on him.'

Bayern were disposed of by goals from Sandy Jardine and debutant Derek Parlane at Ibrox, and so it was on to Spain on Wednesday May 24, 1972.

Once again injury let Johnstone into the side. Big Colin Jackson picked up a knock in training, and couldn't make the game against the Russians.

'I don't think I would have played if it hadn't been for 'Bomber's' bad luck,' says Johnstone.

Play he did, at centre-half, in what was to be a night that contained the best and worst moments of his footballing life.

It's history that Rangers won 3-2, after leading 3-0 with goals from Colin Stein and a Willie Johnston double. The events that followed made history, too.

Rangers fans, fired by the heat, cheap drink, excitement and anxiety as the Russians fought back to score twice in the second half, invaded the pitch on several occasions in the belief that the final whistle had gone. Then of course there were the desperate scenes of battle as the affair got out of hand and became a police v supporters confrontation.

'I nearly suffocated in the crush at the end,' says Derek.

'The fans, who had pawned the telly to be there in their thousands, wanted souvenirs. They were trying to rip the shirt and shorts off us.'

'In fact, I would have lost my jersey if it hadn't been for the fact that I spotted a pal of mine from Dundee.'

'I whipped off my strip and he stuffed it up his jumper. Otherwise I would never have saved it.'

'As it was I was left with only my 'Y' fronts. And there were fingermarks on them as well!'

'What should have been the greatest night of my career, became my biggest disappointment. We couldn't be presented with the trophy, and instead John Greig received it in a wee room 8 ft by 6ft under the stand with the rest of us in the bath.'

A satisfied Derek Johnstone after yet another Rangers goal.

Disappointing, yes. But Johnstone still points out that the Waddell-Wallace team of 1972 did what the great sides of the '50s and '60s failed to do . . . land a European trophy.

'They might have had better players, but they never had a team with the spirit of the '70s,' says Derek.

'We all worked our guts out for the side, and never admitted defeat. The team spirit was akin to the kind of set-up Hearts have right now, with a terrific 'feel' in the dressing room.'

And, of course, there was Jock Wallace who was to step up after Barcelona to become manager with Waddell concentrating on the administration.

'Jock was a tremendous motivator. People try to say he didn't have tactics. But the man won eight trophies in six seasons, including two trebles.'

'He might not speak in Oxford English, but my God he could get through to players.'

Which brings to mind an escapade which still makes Johnstone smile.

As a brash 18-year-old, with a taste for the good life, he

lingered on after the summer break and failed to turn up for training.

'I had met up with some enjoyable company on holiday in Spain, and was invited back to London with them. I was having such a good time, I went. And was still there when training resumed.'

'I don't know how the hell big Jock found out where I was, but there I was in this pub in Chelsea ordering up a round — it always seemed to be my round.'

'Three pints of light, two shandies, a lager . . . I was reciting the order when right across the room came this growl: 'And I'll have a half'.

'I'll tell you, the hairs on the back of my neck stood up. It was big Jock.'

'The sight of this huge, frighteningly strong-looking man with the fierce blue eyes behind the glasses scared the shandy out of me. And everyone else.'

'I was back in Glasgow the next day. And boy did I suffer in training. Mind you, I must admit I was an ounce or two over-weight.'

Johnstone's unfortunate ability to put on weight easily was to become a problem to him later in his career, and even now he carries on a continual battle against the bulge.

But in those leaner, keener days of the 1970s he set about winning Leagues and Cups as well as the admiration of the Ibrox fans.

The League titles: four League Cups and five Scottish Cups . . . all came to Johnstone as Rangers broke the domination which Celtic had imposed on Scottish football under Jock Stein.

Johnstone didn't score in the 1973 Scottish Cup victory over Celtic . . . but set up the winner which came from the unlikely figure of sweeper Tom Forsyth.

'I hit the post with a header from a Tommy McLean free kick, and big Tam just got his foot to the rebound to push it home.'

'We couldn't catch him as he ran up the field celebrating. That's the fastest he ever moved. I always maintain that if he had been wearing short studs he would have missed the ball.'

Johnstone spent most of that season in defence, but still totted up ten competitive goals.

Rangers swept to their first League success in thirteen years in 1974-75, the last before Premier football came to Scotland. They finished seven points clear of Hibs, with Johnstone scoring fourteen League goals . . . three fewer than Derek Parlane.

The title was taken by six points again in the first of the new Premier Divisions in 1975-76. And so were both the Scottish and League Cups as Rangers hit the treble trail.

Johnstone contributed 31 competitive goals, including a double against Motherwell in the Scottish Cup semi-final at Hampden when Rangers trailed 2-0 . . . and followed this with two more in the 3-1 victory over Hearts in the Final.

The next year's final brought Celtic a controversial winner, scored from the penalty spot by Andy Lynch in the 20th minute.

Johnstone was the unfortunate offender — although he maintains to this day that a shot from big Icelander Johannes Edvaldsson actually hit him on the thigh, and he didn't handle.

'Celtic claimed just as we would have done — and although referee Bob Valentine was unsighted, he gave the award.'

'I still say he made a mistake.'

Season 1977-78 will undoubtedly go down as the golden year for Johnstone.

He won the treble with Rangers, was voted Player of the Year, and scored a total of 38 goals in major competitions. This included a hat-trick against Motherwell and what turned out to be the winner in the 2-1 Scottish Cup Final over Aberdeen.

He also scored twice for Scotland inside four days as the Scots drew with Ireland and Wales at Hampden. His headed goal against the Welsh from fifteen yards is still rated one of the best seen at Hampden.

However, he was also ordered off in that season in a European tie against Young Boys in Berne . . . just a year after suffering the same fate in another Euro tie in Zürich.

There must have been something in the Swiss air which sent him cuckoo. Now that's the kind of joke he enjoys.

When Jock Wallace suddenly resigned after his treble triumph, John Greig stepped straight from the dressing room to the manager's room.

It was a popular move at the time, but it proved not to be successful in the long run as the man who was Rangers' greatest captain failed to find the same success in his off-field role.

Greig named Johnstone as his successor as captain — a move that was to prove disastrous for both of them. Their relationship had soured by the time Johnstone eventually left to join Chelsea five years later.

Greig was to say on his own departure from Ibrox that making Johnstone captain was the worst mistake he had made.

And even now in their parallel careers in broadcasting, where they meet frequently, their relationship is still ill at ease.

Greig clearly felt Johnstone failed to do justice to the job as captain. Johnstone maintains he didn't want the job in the first place but was told he was 'the only man to do it'.

'I asked four or five times to be relieved of the job because I thought my form was suffering. But I was told to battle through.'

Yet, at the start it looked as though the new set-up would work.

In that first season, Johnstone held two Cups aloft in triumph, the League Cup won in March — postponed because of the bad winter — with a 2-1 win over Aberdeen, and seven weeks later the Scottish Cup taken after three gruelling matches against Hibs.

Johnstone played a major role in the Hampden Finals. Against Hibs in the second replay he scored twice in the 3-2 win, although the crucial winning goal was a cruel own goal by Hibs winger Arthur Duncan who headed past his own keeper in the 20th minute of extra time.

Derek's part in the League Cup Final was much more controversial.

Starting out at centre-half, he was moved up into attack after Duncan Davidson had put Dons ahead in the 59th minute.

A word in your ear — Johnstone with Celtic centre-half Tom McAdam as they jostle before a corner.

He had hardly moved upfield than he went down flat on his face — poleaxed by a tackle from behind by Aberdeen's giant defender Doug Rougvie.

Referee Ian Foote immediately sent Rougvie off, and Johnstone was accused by Aberdeen players of cheating and faking the foul.

'You would have thought Rougvie was a choirboy the way they went on,' says Derek. 'I was pilloried in the Press and radio up north, but Rangers would never let me answer back. Eventually Dons were reprimanded for some of their remarks.'

'The plain truth is that Rougvie DID hit me in the back with his knee. Anyone who has any doubts should read referee Foote's version from the book he published when he retired.'

'He says clearly that he turned round when Peter McCloy launched a big clearance upfield and saw Rougvie hit me in the back.'

That same season Johnstone had the distinction of scoring four goals in the thrilling 5-3 win over Hearts at Ibrox on December 9.

Season 1979-80 was a near disaster for Rangers. They finished fifth in the League, went out of the League Cup to home and away defeats by Aberdeen and were beaten 3-1 at home in the second leg of a Cup Winners Cup second-round tie by Valencia of Spain, with Argentina's World Cup star Kempes scoring twice.

John Greig was busily changing the team round to his way of thinking. Derek Parlane and Gordon Smith left — and bought in were Gregor Stevens from Leicester, Ian Redford from Dundee, Colin McAdam from Partick Thistle and Jim Bett from Belgian club Lokeren.

'Personally I think Greigy tried too much too soon,' says Johnstone.

'He wanted us to play total football, like the great Dutch teams. But it just didn't work, and you don't get a lot of sympathy at Ibrox from anyone when you're not winning. Players were bought when the team was struggling, not when we were still at the top the way Liverpool do it.'

Johnstone was to win one more medal with Rangers — in the 1981 Scottish Cup. But only after being drafted into the side, along with Davie Cooper and John MacDonald, for the replay after the teams had drawn 1-1 with Ian Redford missing a penalty in injury time.

Johnstone didn't score, but played his part in the 4-1 replay success . . . a game dominated by the brilliant Davie Cooper.

'Davie is the most skilful player I've seen in Scottish football. He could do anything with that left foot. I was lucky to play with a lot of good wingers at Ibrox who made scoring easier for me — Willie Henderson, Tommy McLean, Davie Cooper, Willie Johnston.'

By 1981, Johnstone could see little future for him at Ibrox — and asked away. But it wasn't until two years later that he finally did make the break, moving to Chelsea on September 1, 1983 for £30,000.

'I didn't want to leave, really, and would have liked to stay on. Although I didn't fancy reserve football, I thought I could have helped with the coaching of the younger players.'

His move to Chelsea was enjoyable, if not much of a success.

'I only played a handful of First Team games. They had Kerry Dixon and David Speedie as their main strikers — players ten years younger than me and highly priced.'

'But I did enjoy working with the young players there and won a reserve championship medal.'

Derek also achieved an ambition while with Chelsea — he was put on loan for a month to Dundee United so at last got a chance to wear the famous tangerine jersey.

'A fan pointed out to me that the four teams I have played for, Rangers, Chelsea, Dundee United and Scotland all have a lion somewhere in the team crest.'

Johnstone was back at Ibrox in January 1985, brought back for £28,000 by another man making his second appearance with Rangers . . . Jock Wallace, who had been called back as third-choice replacement for Greig after he had resigned in October.

But the old magic was not there. Not for Wallace. Not for Johnstone.

'Jock was still a great character. But the years in England

F

with Leicester had softened his discipline. And, of course, he was older. Plus, of course, he hardly knew many of the players.'

Wallace left on April 7, 1986 . . . replaced in a sensational move by new supremo David Holmes, who went to Italy and persuaded Graeme Souness to quit Sampdoria and take on the role as player-manager at Ibrox.

'I didn't expect to last long after that,' says Derek. And he didn't.

'It was on the cards that Souness would make a clear out.' And he did.

Johnstone was one of a handful of players who left in May.

Within a month he was back in action, as player-coach with Partick Thistle who were under control of his old Chelsea chairman Ken Bates. Within another two weeks he was player-manager when Peter Cormack left.

And eight months after that he was out of a job.

'The least said about Partick Thistle the better,' says Derek. 'It was the worst eight months of my life. Not because of the players. Because of the man who owned the club and the other directors.'

His departure came in a welter of scathing comments from both sides of the divide . . . climaxing in his club car vanishing from the driveway of his Renfrewshire home as Jags spirited it back.

Now he's on to yet another career — broadcaster and writer, and enjoying it. He also enjoys the family life offered by a bustling young family of three daughters and a tearaway toddler son.

He sees a lot of Rangers, of course, and admires what Graeme Souness is setting out to achieve.

'Only he could have brought the big name stars like Woods and Butcher to Ibrox.'

'But he'll have to get the discipline sorted out. They have lost major games simply because too many players were on the sidelines.'

'Rangers will have to take a lesson from Liverpool. Everyone wants to knock them over as well. But their players just get up and walk away from trouble.'

Up for the Cup! Johnstone gives team-mate Bobby Russell a helping hand.

'Souness and Co. know by now they are under special pressures. And there are no walk-overs nowadays.'

Johnstone has only one real 'beef' about his Ibrox days . . . he was never given a testimonial game.

'Others got one. Others are getting one in the future. I was a Rangers player for fifteen seasons. I think that was worthy of similar recognition.'

INTERNATIONAL RECORD

1973			
May	Wales	(a)	2-0
May	N. Ireland	(h)	1-2
May	England	(a)	0-1
June	Switzerland	(a)	0-1
June	Brazil	(h)	0-1

1974			
Oct.	E. Germany	(h)	3-0 sub.
1975			
April	Sweden	(a)	1-1 sub.
1976			
April	Switzerland	(h)	1-0
May	N. Ireland	(h)	3-0 sub.
May	England	(h)	2-1 sub.
1978			
Feb.	Bulgaria	(h)	2-1 sub.
May	N. Ireland	(h)	1-1
May	Wales	(h)	1-1
1979			
Dec.	Belgium	(h)	1-3

He also won six Under-23 caps, and had the distinction of netting Rangers' 6,000th League goal in the 4-0 win over Clyde at Ibrox on March 30th, 1974.

CHAPTER NINE

Ally McCoist

Ally McCoist is already in the record books . . . as Scottish football's eight-day wonder.

That's how long it took him to recover from a cartilage operation and get back in action in the middle of season '87-88.

Now he aims to make another entry into the record lists this season. AS THE HOLDER OF THE RECORD NUMBER OF LEAGUE GOALS FOR RANGERS IN THE POST-WAR YEARS.

Who's a happy boy, then? Ally celebrates a goal against Celtic.

Currently that position is held by Derek Johnstone, who netted 131 League goals in his career at Ibrox.

And when McCoist slammed in the second of his two goals in the 5-0 win against Falkirk at Brockville on May 7, 1988 in Rangers' final League game of the term, he boosted his overall tally to 110.

'Derek's record is there for the taking,' says Ally. 'And there's nothing I would like better than to get it from him.'

'Maybe it would keep him quiet for a while. But knowing him, I doubt that very much. At least it would give me some revenge for the daft tricks he has played on me over the years. Although it would never make up for having to listen to those jokes of his!'

Admittedly, playing in an extended Premier Division, with a 44-game programme, has helped the McCoist cause a lot.

But scoring 34 and then 31 goals in the larger League is still a considerable feat.

'The more the merrier,' says Ally. 'There is nothing quite like it in the world when you hit the back of the net.'

'Quite honestly, it doesn't matter to me how the ball ends up there. It can go in off my bum if it likes. I'll still celebrate just as though I'd banged in a 30-yard spectacular.'

'In fact, some of the lads say that if a ball has passed within two feet of me on its way into the net I'm liable to claim the goal for myself.'

McCoist is a bubbly person on and off the field. There cannot be many more likeable or presentable young men in the game.

You can tell watching him in action as he meets the fans after a game that he is loving every minute of the attention. But in return for their loyalty, he is willing to spend as much time as they like signing autographs and posing for pictures.

'Life is all about fun, as far as I'm concerned,' says the 26-year-old striker. 'I'm thoroughly enjoying myself.'

'I love football. I never wanted to be anything else but a player.'

'To have reached the top level at club and international standing is something I cherish.'

But although his zest for living ensures that he is never down for long, Ally admits that he takes his football so seriously that he quite often ends up in tears.

'If I'm really uptight about a game, and we don't get the result I wanted or I've missed a couple of vital chances, then I can finish up sitting in the dressing room crying.'

Apart from Derek Johnstone's goal record, Ally has set himself other targets to aim for.

'Like a Scottish Cup medal for a start,' he says. 'In my five seasons with Rangers since I joined them in June 1983, we have never got past the fifth round of the Cup.'

'It has been totally frustrating. And included in the disappointments have been the Hamilton Accies stunner and that exit against Dunfermline.'

'I'd like to put that record right as soon as possible.'

Dundee were one of the teams to give Rangers the Cup elbow, dumping them two seasons in succession.

'I won't forget the game at Ibrox where they beat us 1-0,' says Ally.

'I was going through a bad patch with the club at the time and the fans were giving me some stick. The chants from the Copland Road stand were even louder that day.'

'I must have had about ten chances and missed them all.'

'They were going over the bar, past the post, hitting the keeper.'

It was so bad that the Dundee scorer that day, John Brown — now with Rangers, of course — went over to McCoist and said: 'I can't believe this is happening to you, Ally.'

'John and I played in the same school select together for East Kilbride and District,' says Ally. 'But it wasn't sympathy I needed. It was goals.'

Indeed, matters were so bad at that point that he lost his first-team place and seemed poised for another move.

'I was told one day by Jock Wallace, who had taken over as manager a few months earlier, that he would keep me informed of any moves.'

'It was a bit shattering. I went home, thought about it all night and went to him next day and told him I didn't want to leave. It had taken me a long time to get to Ibrox, and I still believed I could make it with Rangers.'

He was proved right. His form improved. The goals came. And so did full Scotland honours, the first of which was against Holland in April 1986.

Ally has come a long way since his days as a boy in his home town of East Kilbride when his ambition to be a foot-baller — and a Rangers player — was fired at the age of six or seven when he won a football competition in the now defunct Glasgow *Evening Citizen.*

'The prize was a football strip of your choice. I chose Rang-ers, and I never took the jersey off for weeks,' he recalls.

Yet despite his affection for the Light Blue jersey, Ally twice turned down a chance to wear it for real before he finally ended up with Rangers.

As a schoolboy at Hunter High, and also starring with Fir Park Boys Club, he had a chance to go and train at Ibrox.

'Motherwell wanted me as well. The manager then was Roger Hynd.'

'But all I was being offered was an 'S' form signing. And I've never been in favour of that particular route to the top. I don't know why. Just a personal feeling about it.'

Which is where ex-referee Alex McClintock from Bishop-briggs comes on the scene. Alex at that time was scout for St. Johnstone, and very successful too. Over the years he took players like John Connolly, Jim Pearson and Gordon Smith . . . all of whom like McCoist were transferred to England for con-siderable sums.

'I knew that Ally didn't want to be an 'S' signing. Even at the age of 16 he was confident enough in his own ability to demand being taken on as a senior player,' says Alex.

'I don't think our manager at the time, Alex Stuart, thought we had a hope of signing him. So much so that it was me who got the job of taking the form to the McCoist home.'

He also took a wee bunch of flowers for Mrs McCoist, which may have helped.

'But it was the promise of first-team football at an early date that lured me,' says Ally.

The sweet smile of success.

He was 16 when he joined Saints on December 1, 1978. He was still 16 when he made his debut against Raith Rovers on April 7, 1979 in a 3-0 win and had three more games in succession as Saints 'blooded' this talented youngster.

He played thirteen times the following year, and was learning all the time.

'I used to leave for Perth straight from school for training two nights a week,' says Ally. 'It was nearly midnight before I got home again.'

'But it was thoroughly enjoyable. The train journey up from Glasgow with experienced pros like John Brogan, John Pelosi and Don McNeill was a learning experience.'

This covered all aspects of the life of a footballer — including the traditional 'wind up.'

'The very first trip I made by train, big Jackie O'Brien quizzed me: 'Do you like a drink, son?'

'Don't drink,' I said.

'How about a smoke, then?'

'Don't smoke,' I said.

'Do you fancy the women, then?'

'Not really,' I said.

'Big Jackie looked at me for a minute, then asked:

'Do you make your own dresses?'

That was Ally initiated into the hard, but often humorous, lifestyle of a professional footballer.

Over the years since, Ally has become a collector of footballing anecdotes, and loves to tell them.

One of his favourites was told to him by big Jock Wallace, and concerned much-criticised Ibrox full back Jim Denny.

'Big Jock sent Denny on to warm up as substitute during a game against Celtic, and couldn't understand it when Jim went to the end where the Celtic fans were to do his exercises.'

'What did you do that for?' he demanded. Denny said: 'Boss, I get less stick up that end.'

The legendary Wallace featured again in another tale — this time involving Ally.

'Big Jock was strict about us getting back in our hotel at the laid-down time. During one trip to Switzerland I was still outside the hotel talking at the curfew time.'

'Jock came thundering out, and ordered me up to my room telling me he'd be up to see me. I was quaking.'

'My room-mate Cammy Fraser was, as usual, sitting up in bed watching the telly smoking a big cigar. When I told him what had happened, he told me not to worry, big Jock wouldn't do anything.'

'Then came a thump at the door, with Jock demanding to be let in. Cammy nonchalantly got out of bed, cigar in hand and strolled across the room. I thought he was going to open the door.'

'Instead he disappeared into the bathroom and locked the door! I went to let Jock in — and when I did he promptly belted me one on the chin. Obviously it wasn't a full blow, or I might not be here to tell the story. But I was certainly never late back again.'

Ally is following in the footsteps of Derek Johnstone as the Ibrox dressing-room joker.

If all the socks are swapped round in different shoes — blame Ally.

If there is Algipan — a deep heat ointment — in someone's underpants, blame Ally.

Iain Ferguson, the £1 million signing from St Mirren, was a victim of the hot pants on his first day at Ibrox, with the dressing room in silent stitches as the clearly discomfited Fergie became more and more agitated while trying to remain non-chalant at the same time.

Even manager Graeme Souness has fallen victim . . . albeit by mistake.

'I had bought a bar of trick soap which looked normal but actually gave off a black froth,' says Ally. 'It was meant for assistant manager Walter Smith, so you can imagine how I felt when I was summoned to the manager's private shower room for a severe ticking off on some matter.'

There he was lecturing me severely, but slowly getting blacker and blacker. I couldn't stop myself laughing. Fortunately he did as well when he dicovered the cause of the hilarity.'

Ally learned his tricks of the trade from seasoned players at St. Johnstone. Then Sunderland. And finally Rangers.

He has crammed a lot into his 26 years. He was still only 18 when he was pitched into the big time of English football as a £400,000 wonder boy.

He shot to stardom in one spectacular season . . . 1980-81. He scored his first of 23 goals for St Johnstone in a 3-0 win over Dumbarton at Boghead on August 16, 1980.

And the Scotsport cameras were at Perth — taking in curling at the ice rink the next day — when he slammed in four goals in a 6-2 win over Berwick Rangers on March 21, 1981.

'That was a bit special,' says Ally. 'It was a lucky break the cameras being there in the first place. And to get four goals was unbelievable.'

There was no way Saints could hold on to this hot property. And after he opened season '81-82 with goals in League Cup ties against opposition like Hibs, Celtic and St Mirren the big clubs pounced.

'St Johnstone had offers from Rangers, Sunderland, Wolves and Middlesbrough.'

'I spoke to John Greig at Ibrox, then with manager Alex Rennie and Chairman Alex Lamond, and my father went to see the other clubs.'

'My dad simply said to me: 'You can't make a mistake, no matter what you do. It's like having four great presents, but you're only allowed to take one of them.'

Ally went for the package wrapped in the red and white of Sunderland. They offered £100,000 more than Rangers, so it was easy to see why St Johnstone steered him in the direction of Wearside rather than Clydeside.

'I wanted to do well at Sunderland, but it never worked out,' recalls Ally.

'The club were never out of the bottom four. It was always a struggle and there was a bad atmosphere at times caused by boardroom squabbles.'

'But I did gain invaluable experience. Played at some of the great grounds in England and both with and against tremendous players.'

Ally battling for the ball against Rangers in his St. Johnstone days.

'I beat Peter Shilton with a great overhead kick in a game against Southampton. Faced up to Kenny Dalglish at Liverpool and learned a lot from playing with men like Leighton James and Frank Worthington.'

'I have some good memories. And the fans were great. I still get letters from them to this day.'

But he never did as well as he hoped, scoring only nine goals in his two seasons at Roker Park. Family problems back home in East Kilbride affected him deeply as well, so when the chance came to join Rangers, Ally knew it was third time lucky.

'Sunderland manager Alan Durban was very honest with me. He told me to go, since he himself might not be at the club for long. He was right on both counts.'

McCoist met up with Ibrox boss Greig and his assistant Tommy McLean in the Crest Hotel in Carlisle . . . and finally became a Rangers player.

It cost Rangers £185,000 to sign him on June 8, 1983.

Ally's favourite memory of the event is phoning his granny in Thornliebank to tell her the news, to be told: 'About time, too.'

He made his competitive debut on August 20, 1983 in the 1-1 draw with St Mirren at Ibrox in the Premier League, a game in which Paisley winger Iain Scanlon was ordered off.

He scored his first goal for the club a week later, the last in a 4-1 win over Queen of the South in a League Cup second-leg tie at Palmerston.

The League Cup was to bring Ally his first major medal in his first season with Rangers.

By the time Rangers reached the final against Celtic at Hampden on March 25, 1984 they had twice beaten Q.O.S., Clydebank, Hearts and St Mirren in section games. Then added two semi-final wins home and away against Dundee United.

In that run of ten games Rangers had scored 29 goals, with Ally netting six of them. Better was to follow, for if he didn't single-handedly beat Celtic before 66,369 fans at Hampden . . . he scored all three goals in the 3-2 extra-time victory.

'It was an amazing game,' says Ally. 'My first Hampden final and totally unforgettable.'

'I scored from the penalty spot to put us in front just before half-time, and then got a second in the 61st minute. Celtic looked dead and buried — but they rose from the grave to score first through Brian McClair then equalised with a Mark Reid penalty in the last minute of normal time.'

'The edge really lay with Celtic then.'

But the drama wasn't over for Rangers — or McCoist. He was sent crashing by Celtic skipper Roy Aitken, and got up to take the resultant penalty himself.

Another war dance as Ally scores again.

Celtic's Pat Bonner saved the kick — but a relieved Ally found time to follow up to net the winner from the rebound.

The teams that day were:

Rangers: McCloy; Nicholl, Dawson; McClelland, Paterson, McPherson; Russell, McCoist, Clark (McAdam), MacDonald (Burns), Cooper.

Celtic: Bonner; McGrain, Reid; Aitken, McAdam, MacLeod; Provan (Sinclair), P. McStay, McGarvey (Melrose), Burns, McClair.

That was the only high-note for Ally in that first season. Five months after John Greig signed him, Greig gave up as Rangers boss, and after first of all Alex Ferguson and Jim McLean had turned down the post, back came Jock Wallace.

Ally's first season ended with nine League goals and the same again in the League Cup. Rangers also contrived to run up an 18-0 aggregate score against Valetta of Malta in the Cup Winners Cup . . . with McCoist failing to contribute. He certainly missed the 10-0 home victory, but in the 8-0 first-leg victory the scoring went to defender David McPherson who popped in four.

Ally confesses: 'It took me a lot longer to settle at Ibrox than I expected. About two years I reckon, and I was nearly on my way in the middle of all that.'

'I had to learn the hard way just how difficult life is for a Rangers striker on the field. And just as awkward off the field, too.'

'A couple of escapades on a night out brought me a lot of publicity I didn't want. But I've learned now to stay clear of the problem places.'

'I blame most of it on drink. Young guys get fired up, think they are John Wayne and start trying to pick on anyone they think might be a celebrity of some kind.'

'It was just as hard on the pitch. If the goals dried up, the fans and the critics opened up. Still, I hear I'm in good company. Jim Forrest apparently scored 54 goals in one season and wasn't fancied!'

What probably hasn't helped McCoist over the years has

Never mind the weather — there's a goal to celebrate!

been the revolving door syndrome at Ibrox which has seen strikers in for a whirl and out again.

'I reckon I must have played with about fourteen or fifteen different partners in my years at Ibrox.' says Ally.

A quick check can confirm he has teamed up over the

years with Sandy Clark, John MacDonald, Davie Mitchell, Bobby Williamson, Eric Ferguson, Iain Ferguson, Derek Johnstone, Robert Fleck, Colin West, Marc Falco, Ian Durrant, Ian Ferguson plus sundry others who have all had a wee spin on the roundabout.

'I must confess that I miss Robert Fleck. He was a great foil for me, and I was sorry to lose him as a partner when he was transferred to Norwich.'

However, Ally is gaining in experience himself with every passing season and now takes the ups and downs, and the in-and-out appearances of colleagues, as part of the game.

'I know now not to worry if I'm missing a chance or two. At least I'm always in the position to have a go and in other games I'll get my share.'

He does, too. Which makes it more surprising at times when manager Graeme Souness comes with hints, or even obvious criticism of his No. 1 striker.

The problem is probably that Souness compares every striker to the brilliant Ian Rush, with whom he starred in the Liverpool team.

'I can recall the boss telling me in one game, where I had a poor match but scored a couple of goals, that he had played with Rush when the striker had a real stinker of a day . . . and still scored a hat-trick.'

'Still, it's no bad thing to set your sights on being as close to Ian Rush as you can.'

There is no doubt that in the past year or so, McCoist has added an extra dimension to his game — aggression.

'I don't go looking for trouble, but I can mix it with the big fellows in defence if that's what they want,' he says.

He showed that in his comeback against Steua Bucharest right after his cartilage operation.

'I knew I was going to get a few whacks off their big defender Bombescu, so I decided I would get in a few myself right away just to let him know I wasn't scared.'

'After a couple of times he looked at me, pointed to his head and said in broken English: 'You f----- crazy, yes!' I just nodded in agreement.'

A holding operation — Ally and Aberdeen's Robert Connor get to grips.

That cartilage op is still one of the game's great talking points.

Ally reveals a few of the details: 'I went in to Ross Hall hospital at 5.30 one night for the operation, which was done by a new technique which just leaves two little pin holes in your leg. A bit like a bite from Dracula, in fact!'

'I didn't sleep all night. Not because of any pain, but I was determined to start remedial exercises straight away so I whiled away the night hours doing some leg work.'

'Do you know, I walked out the hospital at 8.30 the following morning without a limp.'

Ally recounted this story to me at the last Scottish Football Writers Association dinner to celebrate Player of the Year (Paul McStay in this case).

And listening in sheer bewilderment was big Willie Wood-burn, who recalled his own six or seven-week lay-off for a simi-lar operation in his playing days.

'I didn't feel any reaction, but obviously I must have lost a little bit of sharpness over the next few weeks,' says Ally.

Now he looks forward to new challenges. Like getting that scoring record from Johnstone; winning a Scottish Cup; tak-ing the League again; and getting a European medal.

And as much as anything, playing for Scotland in the World Cup.

'That must be every player's ambition. It's certainly mine.'

'I love playing for Scotland. It wouldn't matter if we were meeting Pakistan or New Guinea — to me it is still a thrill to wear the jersey of my country.'

'I find international football very enjoyable. I don't feel I'm marked as tightly as I am in a club game with Rangers. Pro-bably because there are so many other high-quality players who have to be looked after as well by the opposition.'

'You get more space — but probably fewer chances. I've missed a few for Scotland, but I always feel I can score.'

His best to date was the double he hit in the 2-0 win over Hungary at Hampden on September 9, 1987. When this was followed with a goal in the 2-0 victory over Belgium he was hailed as the answer to Scotland's striking problems.

'It would be nice to think I could get a few for Scotland. But there is a lot of competition for the places.'

'However, you can be sure of one thing — I'll always give it my best effort.'

While on the subject of best efforts, Ally reckons that of all the goals he has scored over the years, the most memorable was for Rangers in the European Cup tie against Kiev at Ibrox in September 1987.

'I've never known an atmosphere like it. You would have thought there was 144,000 in the place rather than 44,000. When I got what turned out to be the winner the place went crazy. The last five minutes was played in a crescendo of singing.'

But that wasn't his best goal. That came against Aberdeen

Ally at his most dangerous — in and around the penalty box.

at Pittodrie when he turned Willie Miller — 'not an easy task,' says Ally — and swept in what he thought was a magnificent effort.

'I did my usual demented bit of celebration and was over at the dug-out showing my delight when Ian Durrant came up and slapped me on the face.'

'Behave yourself, Coisty. You're no' getting it,' he said.'

'I couldn't believe it. The goal was ruled out for offside against someone else.'

He also recalls scoring a brilliant goal against Kuwait in Jordan.

'There wasn't a damn soul there, but I still did my usual celebration act. You've got to keep in practice, you know!'

It's this irrepressible touch that won Ally the BBC Sport-scene Personality of the Year Award in 1987.

There's no doubt he is a personality player. An attractive, likeable personality.

Rangers Facts

League Champions (38 times)
1891* 1899 1900 1901 1902 1911 1912 1913 1918 1920 1921 1923 1924
1925 1927 1928 1929 1930 1931 1933 1934 1935 1937 1939 1947 1949
1950 1953 1956 1957 1959 1961 1963 1964 1975 1976 1978 1987.
* In 1891 the Championship was shared with Dumbarton.

Scottish Cup Winners (24 times)
1894 1897 1898 1903 1928 1930 1932 1934 1935 1936 1948 1949 1950
1953 1960 1962 1963 1964 1966 1973 1976 1978 1979 1981.
The Cup was withheld in 1909 after two drawn games with Celtic, owing to a
riot.

Scottish League Cup Winners (15 times)
1947 1949 1961 1962 1964 1965 1971 1976 1978 1979 1982 1984 1985
1987 1988.

European Cup Winners Cup Winners
1972

Scottish Cup-Winning Teams
1947-48 (beat Morton 1-0, after a 1-1 draw)
Brown; Young, Shaw; McColl, Woodburn, Cox; Rutherford, Thornton, Williamson, Duncanson, Gillick.
1948-49 (beat Clyde 4-1)
Brown; Young, Shaw; McColl, Woodburn, Cox; Waddell, Duncanson,
Thornton, Williamson, Rutherford.
1949-50 (beat East Fife 3-0)
Brown; Young, Shaw; McColl, Woodburn, Cox; Rutherford, Findlay, Thornton, Duncanson, Rae.
1952-53 (beat Aberdeen 1-0, after a 1-1 draw)
Niven; Young, Little; McColl, Woodburn, Pryde; Waddell, Grierson, Simp-
son, Paton, Hubbard.
1959-60 (beat Kilmarnock 2-0)
Niven; Caldow, Little; McColl, Paterson, Stevenson; Scott, McMillan, Millar,
Baird, Wilson.
1961-62 (beat St Mirren 2-0)
Ritchie; Shearer, Caldow; Davis, McKinnon, Baxter; Henderson, McMillan,
Millar, Brand, Wilson.

1962-63 (beat Celtic 3-0 after a 1-1 draw)
Ritchie; Shearer, Provan; Greig, McKinnon, Baxter; Henderson, McMillan, Millar, Brand, Wilson.
1963-64 (beat Dundee 3-1)
Ritchie; Shearer, Provan; Greig, McKinnon, Baxter; Henderson, McLean, Millar, Brand, Wilson.
1965-66 (beat Celtic 1-0 after 0-0 draw)
Ritchie; Johansen, Provan; Greig, McKinnon, Millar; Henderson, Watson, McLean, Johnston, Wilson.
1972-73 (beat Celtic 3-2)
McCloy; Jardine, Mathieson; Greig, Johnstone, MacDonald; McLean, Forsyth, Parlane, Conn, Young. Substitute: Smith (not used).
1975-76 (beat Hearts 3-1)
McCloy; Miller, Greig; Forsyth, Jackson, MacDonald; McKean, Hamilton (Jardine), Henderson, McLean, Johnston. Other Substitute: Parlane (not used).
1977-78 (beat Aberdeen 2-1)
McCloy; Jardine, Greig; Forsyth, Jackson, MacDonald; McLean, Russell, Johnstone, Smith, Cooper (Watson). Other Substitute: Robertson (not used).
1978-79 (beat Hibernian 3-2 after 0-0 and 0-0 draws)
McCloy; Jardine, Dawson (Miller); Johnstone, Jackson, Watson; McLean (Smith), Russell, Parlane, MacDonald, Cooper.
1980-81 (beat Dundee United 4-1 after a 0-0 draw)
Stewart; Jardine, Dawson; Stevens, Forsyth, Bett; Cooper, Russell, Johnstone, Redford, J. MacDonald. Substitutes: McLean and McAdam (not used).

Scottish League Cup-Winning Teams
1946-47 (beat Aberdeen 4-0)
Brown; Young, Shaw; McColl, Woodburn, Rae; Rutherford, Gillick, Williamson, Thornton, Duncanson.
1948-49 (beat Raith Rovers 2-0)
Brown; Young, Shaw; McColl, Woodburn, Cox; Gillick, Paton, Thornton, Duncanson, Rutherford.
1960-61 (beat Kilmarnock 2-0)
Niven; Shearer, Caldow; Davis, Paterson, Baxter; Scott, McMillan, Millar, Brand, Wilson.
1961-62 (beat Hearts 3-1 after a 1-1 draw)
Ritchie; Shearer, Caldow; Davis, Baillie, Baxter; Scott, McMillan, Millar, Brand, Wilson.
1963-64 (beat Morton 5-0)
Ritchie; Shearer, Provan; Greig, McKinnon, Baxter; Henderson, Willoughby, Forrest, Brand, Watson.

1964-65 (beat Celtic 2-1)
Ritchie; Shearer, Caldow; Greig, McKinnon, Wood; Brand, Millar, Forrest; Baxter, Johnston.

1970-71 (beat Celtic 1-0)
McCloy; Jardine, Miller; Conn, McKinnon, Jackson; Henderson, MacDonald, D. Johnstone, Stein, W. Johnston. Substitute: Fyfe (not used).

1975-76 (beat Celtic 1-0)
Kennedy; Jardine, Greig; Forsyth, Jackson, MacDonald; McLean, Stein, Parlane, Johnstone, Young. Substitutes: McKean and Miller (not used).

1977-78 (beat Celtic 2-1)
Kennedy; Jardine, Greig; Forsyth, Jackson, MacDonald; McLean, Hamilton (Miller), Johnstone, Smith, Cooper (Parlane).

1978-79 (beat Aberdeen 2-1)
McCloy; Jardine, Dawson; Johnstone, Jackson, MacDonald; McLean, Russell, Urquhart (Miller), Smith, Cooper (Parlane).

1981-82 (beat Dundee United 2-1)
Stewart; Jardine, Miller; Stevens, Jackson, Bett; Cooper, Russell, Johnstone, J. MacDonald, Dalziel (Redford). Other Substitute: Mackay (not used).

1983-84 (beat Celtic 3-2)
McCloy; Nicholl, Dawson; McClelland, Paterson, McPherson; Russell, McCoist, Clark (McAdam), J. MacDonald (Burns), Cooper.

1984-85 (beat Dundee United 1-0)
McCloy; Dawson, McLelland; Fraser, Paterson, McPherson; Russell (Prytz), McCoist, Ferguson (Mitchell), Redford, Cooper.

1986-87 (beat Celtic 2-1)
Woods; Nicholl, Munro; Fraser (McFarlane), Dawson, Butcher; Ferguson, McMinn, McCoist (Fleck), Durrant, Cooper.

1987-88 (beat Aberdeen on penalties after 3-3 and a.e.t.)
Walker; Nicholl, Munro; Roberts, Gough, McGregor (Cohen); D. Ferguson (Francis), Fleck, McCoist, Durrant, Cooper.

Rangers Scottish League Record

Years	Pld	Won	Lost	Drn	For	Agst	Pts
1890-91	18	13	2	3	58	25	29†
1891-92	22	11	9	2	59	46	24
1892-93	18	12	2	4	41	27	28
1893-94	18	8	6	4	44	30	20
1894-95	18	10	6	2	41	26	22
1895-96	18	11	3	4	57	39	26
1896-97	18	11	4	3	64	30	25
1897-98	18	13	2	3	71	15	29

Years	Pld	Won	Lost	Drn	For	Agst	Pts
1898-99	18	18	0	0	79	18	36*
1899-1900	18	15	1	2	69	27	32*
1900-01	20	17	2	1	60	25	35*
1901-02	18	13	3	2	43	29	28*
1902-03	22	12	5	5	56	30	29
1903-04	26	16	4	6	80	33	38
1904-05	26	19	4	3	83	28	41
1905-06	30	15	8	7	58	48	37
1906-07	34	19	8	7	69	33	45
1907-08	34	21	5	8	74	40	50
1908-09	34	19	8	7	91	38	45
1909-10	34	20	8	6	70	35	46
1910-11	34	23	5	6	90	34	52*
1911-12	34	24	7	3	86	34	51*
1912-13	34	24	5	5	76	41	53*
1913-14	38	27	6	5	79	31	59
1914-15	38	23	11	4	74	47	50
1915-16	38	25	7	6	87	39	56
1916-17	38	24	9	5	68	32	53
1917-18	34	25	3	6	66	24	56*
1918-19	34	26	3	5	86	16	57
1919-20	42	31	2	9	106	25	71*
1920-21	42	35	1	6	91	24	76*
1921-22	42	28	4	10	83	26	66
1922-23	38	23	6	9	67	29	55*
1923-24	38	25	4	9	72	22	59*
1924-25	38	25	3	10	76	26	60*
1925-26	38	19	13	6	79	55	44
1926-27	38	23	5	10	85	41	56*
1927-28	38	26	4	8	109	36	60*
1928-29	38	30	1	7	107	32	67*
1929-30	38	28	6	4	94	32	60*
1930-31	38	27	5	6	96	29	60*
1931-32	38	28	5	5	118	42	61
1932-33	38	26	2	10	113	43	62*
1933-34	38	30	2	6	118	41	66*
1934-35	38	25	8	5	96	46	55*
1935-36	38	27	4	7	110	43	61
1936-37	38	26	3	9	88	32	61*
1937-38	38	18	7	13	75	49	49
1938-39	38	25	4	9	112	55	59*
1946-47	30	21	5	4	76	26	46*
1947-48	30	21	5	4	64	28	46

Years	Pld	Won	Lost	Drn	For	Agst	Pts
1948-49	30	20	4	6	63	32	46*
1949-50	30	22	2	6	58	26	50*
1950-51	30	17	9	4	64	37	38
1951-52	30	16	5	9	61	31	41
1952-53	30	18	5	7	80	39	43*
1953-54	30	13	9	8	56	35	34
1954-55	30	19	8	3	67	33	41
1955-56	34	22	4	8	85	27	52*
1956-57	34	26	5	3	96	48	55*
1957-58	34	22	7	5	89	49	49
1958-59	34	21	5	8	92	51	50*
1959-60	34	17	9	8	72	38	42
1960-61	34	23	6	5	88	46	51*
1961-62	34	22	5	7	84	31	51
1962-63	34	25	2	7	94	28	57*
1963-64	34	25	4	5	85	31	55*
1964-65	34	18	8	8	78	35	44
1965-66	34	25	4	5	91	29	55
1966-67	34	24	3	7	92	31	55
1967-68	34	28	1	5	93	34	61
1968-69	34	21	6	7	81	32	49
1969-70	34	19	8	7	67	40	45
1970-71	34	16	9	9	58	34	41
1971-72	34	21	11	2	71	38	44
1972-73	34	26	4	4	74	30	56
1973-74	34	21	7	6	67	34	48
1974-75	34	25	3	6	86	33	56*
1975-76	36	23	5	8	60	24	54*
1976-77	36	18	8	10	62	37	46
1977-78	36	24	5	7	76	39	55*
1978-79	36	18	9	9	52	35	45
1979-80	36	15	14	7	50	46	37
1980-81	36	16	8	12	60	32	44
1981-82	36	16	9	11	57	45	43
1982-83	36	13	11	12	52	41	38
1983-84	36	15	9	12	53	41	42
1984-85	36	13	11	12	47	38	38
1985-86	36	13	14	9	53	45	35
1986-87	44	31	6	7	85	23	69*
1987-88	44	26	10	8	85	34	60
	2990	1894	517	579	6898	3134	4367

* Champions   † Joint with Dumbarton